GLOBETROTTER™

Travel Guide

INDONESIA

Janet Cochrane
Debbie Martyr

D0539792

NEW
HOLLAND

★★★ Highly recommended
★★ Recommended
★ See if you can

Seventh edition published in 2013
by New Holland Publishers (UK) Ltd
London • Cape Town • Sydney • Auckland
10 9 8 7 6 5 4 3 2 1
website: www.newhollandpublishers.com

Garfield House, 86 Edgware Road
London W2 2EA, United Kingdom

Wembley Square, First Floor, Solan Road
Gardens, Cape Town 8001, South Africa

Unit 1, 66 Gibbes Street, Chatswood
NSW 2067, Australia

218 Lake Road, Northcote
Auckland, New Zealand

Distributed in the USA by
The Globe Pequot Press, Connecticut

ISBN 978 1 78009 389 5

This guidebook has been written by independent
authors and updaters. The information therein repre-
sents their impartial opinion, and neither they nor the
publishers accept payment in return for including in
the book or writing more favourable reviews of any
of the establishments. Whilst every effort has been
made to ensure that this guidebook is as accurate
and up to date as possible, please be aware that the
facts quoted are subject to change, particularly the
price of food, transport and accommodation. The
Publisher accepts no responsibility or liability for any
loss, injury or inconvenience incurred by readers or
travellers using this guide.

Publishing Manager: Thea Grobbelaar
DTP Cartographic Manager: Genené Hart
Editors: Thea Grobbelaar, Carla Zietsman,
Tarryn Berry, Paul Barnett
Updated by: Janet Cochrane
Design and DTP: Nicole Bannister
Cartographers: Tracay-Lee Fredericks, Reneé Spocter,
Carryck Wise, Nicole Bannister
Picture Researchers: Zainoenisa Manuel,
Shavonne Govender
Reproduction by Hirt & Carter (Pty) Ltd, Cape Town
Printed and bound by Craft Print International Ltd,
Singapore

All photographs by **Gerald Cubitt** with the
exception of the following:
Ivan Vdovin/awl-images.com: cover;
Philip Game: pages 16, 55;
Jill Gocher: pages 4, 11, 13, 17, 18, 20 (top), 26, 29,
58, 60, 62, 63, 65, 66, 72, 75, 77, 78, 79, 81.

The publishers, author and photographer
gratefully acknowledge the generous assistance
during the compilation of this book of:
The Directorate General of Tourism, Indonesia
(London and Jakarta). Additional research by
Kelvin Shewry and Andrew Kirkman.

Keep us Current
Information in travel guides is apt to change, which
is why we regularly update our guides. We'd be
grateful to receive feedback if you've noted something we should include in our updates. If you have
new information, please share it with us by writing to
the Publishing Manager, Globetrotter, at the office
nearest to you (addresses on this page). The most
significant contribution to each new edition will
receive a free copy of the updated guide.

Cover: *Borobudur Buddhist temple is a UNESCO
World Heritage Site.*
Title Page: *Fishing boat off Cabuhan, West Java.*

CONTENTS

1
Introducing Indonesia

Most countries offer the foreign visitor an insight into a different culture, but Indonesia, with its dozens of historical influences, offers something dramatically more. The strands of varied customs, religions, legends and modernity are woven into complex patterns that reveal themselves in layers. Visitors with only a few days to spare will find much of colour and vitality to attract them, while those with more time will discover something deeper about the country's subtlety and diversity.

Indonesia has a well-established tourism industry with excellent accommodation and a good travel infrastructure over much of the archipelago. Travel to and around the more remote regions of Papua, Sumatra and Kalimantan is still fairly time-consuming because the roads are not always in great shape, but it is – generally – no longer something that requires the courage and intrepidity of a wilderness explorer! There has been a vast expansion of flight networks, internet communications have made a huge difference to finding out about destinations and booking accommodation, and the comprehensive network of buses and boats help visitors reach the most distant islands and villages.

Sometimes, when a country is transformed in this way, it pays a heavy price in terms of cultural losses. Not so in Indonesia. For every stretch of silver beach filled with sunbathers from nearby luxury hotels there are plenty of villages rich in traditions that date back not just for centuries but for millennia.

◄ *Opposite: As sun sets, a West Javanese fisherman wades to the shore.*

INTRODUCING INDONESIA

Some parts of Indonesia have been connected in the past with continental landmasses. Papua was at one stage linked with Australia, while Sumatra, Kalimantan, Java and Bali were connected to the Southeast Asian mainland in the Ice Ages when sea levels were lower. The ancestors of the Australian Aborigines and the Tasmanians almost certainly reached their territories via these land-bridges. However, Maluku, Nusa Tenggara and Sulawesi have never been connected to a major landmass and as a result their fauna and flora are fascinating and unique.

THE LAND

With an area of about 1,950,000km^2 (just over 750,000 sq miles), the Republic of Indonesia is the largest country in Southeast Asia and the world's largest archipelago. It stretches some 5150km (3200 miles) and includes over 17,500 islands: about 6000 are inhabited. Roughly 70% of the population lives on **Java**, although with an area of 132,187km^2 (51,123 sq miles, approximately the size of England and Wales) this is far from the largest island; the other major islands are **Sumatra** (473,606km^2; 183,166 sq miles) and **Sulawesi** (189,216km^2; 73,179 sq miles), to which must be added **Kalimantan** (539,460km^2; 208,635 sq miles), which is the Indonesian part (about 70%) of the island of Borneo, and **Papua** (421,981km^2; 163,200 sq miles), the Indonesian part (about 50%) of New Guinea.

Indonesian landscapes are often rugged. Shallow seas patterned with coral reefs surround shores of mangrove swamps and coastal plains reaching back to dense rainforest. The mountains and geological structures are mainly volcanic, with many of the volcanoes still active, for this is a region of geological turmoil. Indonesia straddles not two but three of the tectonic plates of the earth's crust, at whose margins there is ceaseless vol-

canic and earthquake activity: this was dramatically and tragically illustrated by the Asian tsunami in December 2004 and other major earthquakes since then: central Java in 2006 and western Sumatra in 2009. New Guinea and the islands around it are on the **Sahul Shelf**, which is properly part of the Australasian plate. Borneo, Java, Bali, Sumatra, Lombok and Nusa Tenggara are on the **Sunda Shelf**, which is part of the Asian continental plate; until the Java Sea formed not much over 10,000 years ago there were land connections between the western islands and the Asian continental landmass. Sulawesi and Maluku belong to the same geological unit as Japan and the Philippines. The junctions between these plates are marked by deep-sea trenches including the famous **Java Trench**, which is 7450m (24,440ft) deep.

Volcanic Lands

Indonesia is estimated to have 128 active volcanoes. The best known is **Krakatau (Krakatoa)**, a mountainous island between Java and Sumatra whose eruption in 1883 coloured skies worldwide for more than a year and sent tsunamis to ravage neighbouring coastlines. The sound of the explosion was heard nearly 5000km (3000 miles) away. The island was literally blown to bits, but is being slowly rebuilt by continuing volcanism – it's now over 200m (656ft) high.

Other volcanoes of note include **Agung** (in Bali), dormant for nearly a century and a half before its violent eruption in 1963; **Merapi** (near Yogyakarta in Java), whose frequent eruptions add considerably to the agricultural fertility of the soil; **Bromo** (East Java), with its dramatic scenery and fascinating myths; **Galunggung** (in western Java), whose eruption in 1982 sent a mass of ash into the upper atmosphere and nearly swatted a British Airways passenger plane from the sky; and **Kelud** (near Kediri, also in Java), whose ash-flows can mix with the waters of its crater lake to form swiftly moving lahars (mudflows) and where eruptions form dramatic night-time displays.

Despite occasional eruptions, many of the volcanoes are popular with climbers, including **Merapi**, **Semeru** (the highest mountain in Java), **Rinjani** (in Lombok), **Leuser** (in Sumatra) and the twin volcanoes of **Pangrango** and **Gede** (in Java). Most cities and universities have active mountaineering clubs, and in Jakarta there is a mountain-climbing group of expatriates and Indonesians called the Java Lava Club (www.expat.or.id/orgs/javalava.html).

▲ *Above: Looking across the Sunda Straits at sunset.*
◄ *Opposite: Indonesia's landscape has been sculpted by volcanism. This view is across the Sand Sea at Mount Bromo, with Mount Semeru in the distance.*

THE RING OF FIRE

Indonesia lies in one of the world's most volcanically active areas, at the juncture of several tectonic plates, which gives rise to a pattern of volcanic and earthquake activity around the Pacific Ocean and including Japan, New Zealand and the western coast of the Americas.

▲ *Above: A feral buffalo in East Java's Baluran National Park.*

Rivers and Seas

As an island nation, Indonesia has always been dependent upon the sea for transportation and communication, with rivers also important in the interior of the larger landmasses, notably Kalimantan.

The shallow seas around the archipelago are vital as a source of food, and as a base for the tourist industry. As well as the numerous resorts of Bali, Lombok, Bintan and other areas, there is excellent scuba-diving around Sulawesi, East Kalimantan, Maluku, Flores, Komodo and Papua – even the heavily used seas around Java and Bali have some good reefs.

Climate

Indonesia's climate is predominantly tropical, the two main influences being the archipelago's equatorial position and its situation between the landmasses of Australasia and Asia. Such temperature variations as there are depend more on altitude than on geographical location, with the highest average temperatures (21–33°C; 70–90°F) at sea level, but much cooler temperatures in the hills and mountains. There is even a glacier in the high mountains of Papua – and, to great excitement, snow was recorded as falling in a village lying at over 2000m (6500ft) in East Java in 1984.

There are two monsoon seasons. The **East Monsoon** (*musim panas* or hot season) lasts from June to September, and is characterized by dry weather and slightly cooler temperatures, especially in eastern Java and eastwards through the archipelago. Conversely, the **West Monsoon** (*musim hujan* or rainy season) lasts from December to March and brings heavy rainfall, especially in the western archipelago. Even outside the West Monsoon the **rainfall** is generally high in the western islands – Sumatra and Kalimantan do not really have a dry season at all – and the rain can come with terrific intensity over short periods: daily downpours up to 800mm (31in) have been recorded.

The **humidity** is high, generally 75–100%. Afternoon thunderstorms occur frequently all over Indonesia. However, deforestation in the larger islands and global climate change are causing a notable shift in climate patterns, with the rainy season starting later than it used to and many areas receiving less rainfall.

Flora and Fauna

The 19th-century British naturalist Alfred Russel Wallace, who with Charles Darwin realized that the mechanism for evolution was natural selection ('the survival of the fittest'), was the first to note the difference in the flora and fauna of the islands of the Sunda Shelf to the west, including Sumatra, Java, Borneo and Bali, and the islands to the east, including Sulawesi and Lombok. To the west are Asian mammals such as elephants, monkeys, orang-utans, rhinoceroses and tigers, while to the east many of the animals are related to those of Australasia, including marsupials like the kangaroo.

▲ *Above: A green turtle hatchling makes its intrepid way across Sukamade Beach to the sea at Java's Meru Betiri National Park.*

Indonesia has an extremely high level of biodiversity with many species found nowhere else in the world. One of the best known is the **Komodo dragon**, a giant lizard found only on Komodo and Rinca, two islands in the Komodo National Park. Other notable species are the **orang-utan**, native to Sumatra and Kalimantan, the **Sumatran rhinoceros** and the **Javan rhinoceros**, only 50–60 of which survive. The large **Banteng** ox is also a vulnerable species. Kalimantan has the unique **proboscis monkey**, while Sulawesi has several endemics including the boar-like **babirusa** and the **anoa**, a dwarf buffalo.

▼ *Below: A Javan gibbon in Halimun National Park, West Java.*

With over 1500 species of **bird**, including cockatoos and birds-of-paradise in the east, the country is a mecca for bird-watchers – even though it takes tenacity to visit some of the more interesting bird-watching areas. All visitors are certain to be struck by the variety, ubiquity and size of the **insects** and other invertebrates, many of which are beautiful or extraordinary.

SOLO MAN

Java Man (*Homo erectus*) and the tiny *Homo floresiensis* are not the only forms of fossil human to be found in Indonesia: close to where the Java Man bones were discovered were later uncovered a set of cracked-open skulls of what came to be called Solo Man. Solo Man appears to have been not only a prolific hunter – near the skulls were found the remains of a huge collection of animals as well as various hunting and butchering tools – but also, to judge by the evidence of the skulls, a cannibal.

The rainforest has about 40,000 flowering species, from the world's largest flower, *Rafflesia arnoldii*, to tiny orchids. At least 3000 species of tree flourish in the archipelago, many of economic importance, with woods such as teak, ironwood and the pinky-red meranti being valuable commodities. There were estimated to be around 98 million hectares (242 million acres) of forest left in 2002 – but around 2 million hectares (5 million acres) are disappearing every year.

HISTORY IN BRIEF

The human history of Indonesia can be said to date back at least half a million years, for that is the date ascribed to the hominid fossils found in 1891 by Eugène Dubois on the Solo River in Central Java. Java Man, as the remains were called, was originally allotted by the German zoologist Ernst Haeckel to the genus *Pithecanthropus*, meaning 'ape-man'; once it was established that **Java Man** was part of the ancestral tree of modern human beings, *Homo sapiens*, the fossils were reclassified as belonging to the species *Homo erectus*. In 2004 theories of human evolution were rocked when the remains of 18,000-year-old hominids just a metre high were discovered on Flores: the species has been named *Homo floresiensis*.

▼ *Below: Indonesian history seems part of the present. These newly made stone carvings on sale in Bali could have been produced centuries ago.*

Indonesia's history, like everything else about the archipelago, has been profoundly affected by the sea. Waves of human immigration to the islands must have occurred from at least 40,000 years ago, since it is thought that humans reached Australia by travelling through the archipelago – although at that time sea levels were lower and there were land-bridges in place of the tricky currents and channels which exist now. From around 3000BC migration increased, with different groups bringing their languages and customs, echoes of which still survive. For instance,

HISTORICAL CALENDAR

3000BC First waves of immigration by Asian tribes to the archipelago.
AD71 Pliny records Indonesian traders with Africa.
5th cent. Brahman missionaries bring Hinduism to the archipelago.
7th cent. Sriwijaya well established.
8th cent. Sailendra kingdom well established.
c778 onward Borobudur built.
10th cent. Sriwijaya loses trade monopoly with China.
11th cent. Islam arrives in the archipelago.
1268 Kertanagara comes to the throne.
1292 Kertanagara deposed; Marco Polo visits Indonesia.

14th cent. Final extinction of Sriwijayan kingdom.
1602 Dutch East India Company assumes rule of Indonesia.
1799 Dutch East India Company wound up.
1811 British East India Company takes over.
1883 Eruption of Krakatau (Krakatoa).
1891 Discovery of 'Java Man' fossil remains.
1942 Japanese occupation.
1945 Declaration of independence by Sukarno.
1949 Formal transfer of Dutch sovereignty.
1963 Irian Jaya ceded to Indonesia by the Netherlands.

1965–1966 Civil turmoil.
1966 Suharto takes over from Sukarno.
1975 Invasion of East Timor.
Mid-1980s 'Economic liberalization' policies.
1998 Suharto steps down; BJ Habibie becomes president; release of political prisoners; freedom of press.
1999 East Timor regains independence.
1999 President Abdurrachman Wahid elected.
2001 Megawati Sukarnoputri becomes president.
2004 President Susilo Bambang Yudhoyono elected – he was re-elected in **2009** for a further 5 years.

the indigenous tribes of the Mentawaian islands, off the west coast of Sumatra, have cultural similarities with historical groups in Indochina. With different peoples establishing independent settlements all around the coastlines and bringing their own languages, there are now around 580 different languages spoken within Indonesia. The lingua franca – and official language – is Indonesian, or **Bahasa Indonesia**.

By the second century BC trading links with China were established, and gradually trade with other parts of the world developed. The first records of this appear in the works of Pliny the Elder, whose *Historia Naturalis* (begun after AD71) seems to refer to trade between people from Indonesia and the cultures of eastern Africa. There may have been an Indonesian colony on Madagascar by then, and the Malagasy people of today still have physical and linguistic characteristics in common with the Malays of the archipelago. It was about this time that **Hinduism** first came to Indonesia, with the arrival of Indian traders. However, the real impact

▼ Below: The monkey god, Hanuman, in a Balinese performance of the Ramayana.

The national language is Indonesian ('Bahasa Indonesia'). It was adopted in 1928, having been the lingua franca of the archipelago since at least the 15th century. It is basically the same language as Malaysian. There are still living linguistic reminders of the various influences on Indonesia in the form of words derived from Sanskrit, Arabic, Portuguese, Dutch and English.

of Hinduism was to arrive much later, as a deliberate missionary act by Brahmans, probably in the 5th century AD; by a lucky coincidence, some of the basic ideas of Hinduism accorded with existing Indonesian mountain-worship, and a hybrid of the two religions emerged. As Indonesia's major trading partner at that time was southern China, **Buddhist** influences also began to play a part.

Sriwijaya

Until perhaps the 7th century the peoples of the Indonesian islands retained their multiplicity of comparatively small communities, trading and sometimes fighting with each other. Then, a major Buddhist kingdom, Sriwijaya, established itself with its centre just to the west of modern **Palembang**, in Sumatra. The rulers of Sriwijaya amassed considerable wealth as a result of an extensive trade network and use of the region's natural resources. Although the primary religion was Buddhism – largely, it seems, a corrupted form of Tantric Buddhism, using magic for selfish ends – Hindu relics, too, have been excavated from the area, and there is evidence that traditional Malay magical beliefs were also practised.

At the end of the 7th century Sriwijaya moved to conquer the smaller communities along the northeastern coast of Sumatra and thereby monopolize the lucrative trade with China. The maharajahs made various treaties with the natives of smaller islands so that merchant ships could pass unmolested. In this way the kingdom survived until the 10th century, it being convenient for the Chinese to deal with only one centre. However, the Chinese then began trading with local production centres elsewhere in the region, and there was little

▼ Below: Borobudur, built during the late 8th and early 9th centuries, is the world's largest Buddhist monument.

Sriwijaya could do to stop them. The kingdom may have dragged on until sometime in the 14th century, but by then its power was a mere husk.

The Sailendra Princes and the Majapahit Empire

Meanwhile, from about the 8th century, central Java had been ruled by the Sailendra princes. The wealth of their small kingdom was based on agriculture, and they were able to spend lavishly on building religious monuments.

▲ *Above: The temple of Tanah Lot on Bali was built by Sang Hiyang Nirarta, one of the last Javanese missionaries to come to Bali.*

The vast sanctuary and burial edifice of **Borobudur** was built over some 50 years from the end of the 8th century onwards, and the temple complexes at **Prambanan** began to be constructed at about the time that Borobudur was completed.

However, historical records show that at about the start of the 10th century there was a sudden cessation in the creation of monuments, inscriptions and other artefacts in central Java. In eastern Java a series of petty kingdoms rose, fractured and disappeared, thanks to turbulent rulers – rulers rather than commoners, for the commoners seem to have desired a stable kingdom if only for the sake of peace. Yet, despite all this upheaval, eastern Java was extremely wealthy because of continuing trade with China and its fertile soils, and so Java slowly began to assume a dominant position in the archipelago.

In 1268 the Javanese king **Kertanagara** came to the throne, and within a few years had extended his kingdom to include southern Sumatra's ancient kingdom of Malayu. Through overseas contacts he established himself as the pre-eminent ruler in this part of the world. Like local rulers for centuries before him, he assumed the status of divinity, and his cult freely mixed Buddhist and Hindu elements. He was overthrown and killed in 1292 (the year in which **Marco Polo** visited Indonesia), but not before he had – unwisely – sent the envoy of

AN INDUSTRIOUS PRIME MINISTER

The Majapahit Empire reached its peak during the reign of King Hayam Wuruk as a result of the endeavours of his prime minister, Gajah Mada, who dedicated so much energy to uniting the islands of the region that when he died, four men had to take over his functions. Modern historians believe that the empire's boundaries may have been much more circumscribed than was once thought, with outlying territories linked to Majapahit by trade rather than by sovereignty.

Just as the Indonesians had earlier adapted Buddhism to their own needs and beliefs, so they accepted Islam very much on their own terms. The form of Islam that came to the islands had anyway been much changed from that in the religion's cradle in Arabia: it had passed through India and taken on mystical aspects there. Nowadays, a more orthodox form of Islam influenced directly from the Middle East is taking hold: signs of this are the proliferation of substantial, well-funded mosques and increasing social pressure on women to wear conservative clothing.

Kublai Khan home with his nose cut off and 'No' tattooed on his forehead. By the time a punitive Mongol expedition arrived in Java the usurper himself had been despatched by Kertanagara's son-in-law **Kertarajasa**, who used guile to repel the threat from overseas, then set up his new capital at **Trowulan**, in eastern Java. Kertarajasa and his successors gradually established dominance over much of present-day Indonesia as well as parts of Malaysia through the Majapahit empire.

The Growth of Islam

The first Arab traders probably arrived in northern Sumatra around the time of the first millennium, bringing Islam with them. It was a mystical strand of Islam known as Sufism, which accorded well with the existing blend of Hinduism, Buddhism and animism to form a peculiarly idiosyncratic type of Islam. By the end of the 13th century there were two small Islamic kingdoms in northern Sumatra. Over the succeeding two centuries, again because of traders, further Islamic kingdoms spread along the northern shore of Java and around Maluku. The impetus seems to have been entirely commercial: local rulers and their subjects initially converted to the new religion in order to enhance trade with the many Muslim cultures in Asia.

There was no centre of Indonesian Islamic culture from which all else spread; rather there were spontaneous growths of the community here, there and everywhere, forming a mosaic with continuing Hindu strongholds. The scattered nature of the resulting centres of power and influence was to prove a major weakness when the Dutch and other Europeans arrived.

European Rule

Seeking the source of valuable spices, traders from Europe and the Middle East came to Indonesia once ship-building technology allowed them to travel further afield. The Portuguese established a pres-

▼ *Below: Near Banten in West Java, a fortress built by 17th-century sultan and national hero Hasanuddin, who waged a long war against the Dutch.*

ence on the Malay Peninsula early in the 16th century and arrived in Maluku in 1512. They were followed by the British and then the Dutch, who established the **Dutch East India Company** (VOC) in 1602 and effectively governed most of the country until the end of the 18th century through trade and alliances with different rulers. In 1799 the ailing company was wound up by the Dutch Government, its finances deteriorating because of poor management and competing trading links. Control of the country passed to the Dutch government, who held it until independence except for a five-year period (1811–16) when, as a result of European negotiations during the Napoleonic wars, the **British** held the country. **Thomas Stamford Raffles** was appointed Lieutenant Governor and tried to instigate administrative reforms. His system was never put into effect, and the islands reverted to the Dutch after Napoleon's defeat.

The principal interests of the Dutch were still trade-related and despite various rebellions and an increasingly organized local population – especially in Java – they found various means of levying taxes and exploiting their colony's vast natural resources.

▲ *Above:* Bugis pinisi *boats, as used by the first Islamic traders to come to Indonesia, have hardly changed over the centuries E except that they now have engines and cranes to lift the cargo aboard.*

Independence

The country remained in control of the Dutch until 1942, when the Japanese occupied the islands. They proved harsh, exploitative rulers who left a lasting memory of dislike. **Sukarno**, jailed by the Dutch for his nationalist activities, had been freed by the Japanese and made a puppet national leader. On 17 August 1945, just before the Japanese surrendered to the Allies, he and a group of fellow-revolutionaries declared Indonesia independent. The Dutch, however, returned to reclaim their colony. Fierce resistance ensued, until at the end of 1949 the Dutch conceded sovereignty over all of Indonesia except Papua, which was only transferred to Indonesia in 1963.

Sukarno had abundant demagogic skills but lacked political and economic shrewdness. His emphasis on ideology and rejection of ties with the West resulted in economic chaos, and by 1965 inflation was running at

FRIENDS ABROAD

Although the expulsion of the Dutch was a triumph for Indonesia's freedom fighters, their brave efforts were assisted by the pressure other countries brought to bear – particularly the USA, which threatened economic sanctions against the Netherlands. Even so, the struggle for Indonesia's freedom, coming so soon after World War II, was, internationally, very much a forgotten war.

INTRODUCING INDONESIA

THE FIVE PRINCIPLES

The government of Indonesia
has promoted a state ideology
called the Pancasila or five
principles:
• faith in a supreme god
• faith in a just and civilized
humankind
• national pride in the unity
of Indonesia
• democracy (not the parlia-
mentary form of democracy
used by most Western nations
but a system based on discus-
sion, persuasion and consensus)
• social justice, whereby all
citizens have political, cultural
and social equality.

WORLD HERITAGE SITES

Indonesia has eight World
Heritage Sites, inscribed for
their cultural or natural sig-
nificance. The cultural ones
are the ancient temples of
Borobudur and **Prambanan**
and the archaeological site of
Sangiran (all in Java), and – in
2012 – the **rice terrace system
of Bali**. The natural ones are
some of the major national
parks: **Ujung Kulon** (Java),
with the world's last Javan
rhinos; **Komodo**, which protects the Komodo 'dragons'
and fabulous coral reefs;
Lorentz, in Papua; and the
**Tropical Rainforest Heritage
of Sumatra**. More information
at http://whc.unesco.org

over 500% per annum. After what may have been an attempted Communist coup, up to half a million people were killed in violent civil strife during 1965–66. From the chaos emerged a new leader, **General Suharto**, who remained head of the government until 1998. Sukarno was kept under house arrest until his death in 1970. Suharto ended the confrontation with Malaysia that had persisted through the later Sukarno years, took Indonesia back into the United Nations and came to an accommodation with Papua New Guinea, but in 1975 invaded **East Timor**. After considerable loss of life, the territory only regained independence in 1999 after the end of the Suharto regime.

GOVERNMENT AND ECONOMY

During the 1970s and early 80s Indonesia experienced a period of strong economic growth based on its oil and gas reserves and, to a lesser extent, on exploitation of the forests. The country's Western-trained technocrats implemented a centralized planning system which ben-efited most sectors of the population in terms of better health and education and higher incomes. After oil prices fell in the mid-1980s the country was forced to diversify its economy – including an emphasis on tourism. But after increasing levels of nepotism, corrup-tion and economic shocks, Suharto was forced to resign in 1998. Indonesia now describes itself as the third largest democracy in the world. The latest presidential election was in 2009, when President Susilo Bambang Yudhoyono was elected for a second five-year term.

Although economic and social development has been enormous, many peripheral areas have felt excluded, which is one reason for sporadic inter-communal and anti-government violence. An important component of Indonesia's economic growth is the Chinese community, and as a result of their riches they have often been the target of mob violence at times of unrest. A significant source of discontent is now found amongst Islamic groups influenced by a stricter form of Islam emanating from the Middle East. These express their disapproval of the West and un-Islamic behaviour through attacks on Christian villages and churches, although by 2010 social relations between different religious groups had regained much of their former harmony.

There are two legislative houses. The 560 members of the **People's Representative Council** are also members of the **People's Consultative Assembly**, which is augmented by regional representatives. Elections to the Council are held every five years, as with presidential elections.

▲ Above: Rice terraces in Bali. Agriculture is vital to the domestic economy.

Social Welfare

Community health centres have been set up all over the country, though many people still rely on traditional therapies such as herbal medicine (very popular) and shamanistic medicine. **Housing** has been a priority, with the improvement of slum areas and the erection of cheap accommodation for the poor. Education is receiving great emphasis, with schools generally smart and well funded – although there are not enough places for the demand. Private charitable organizations play their part in running **orphanages, schools for the handicapped** and **old people's homes**.

Economy

Oil and **gas** are responsible for about 40% of export revenues, with manufacturing of electrical appliances and clothing also significant. Exploitation of **agricultural** and **forestry** resources such as plywood, rubber and palm oil employ large sectors of the workforce, while other products such as cocoa, coffee, coconuts, spices, tea and tobacco are all grown in huge quantities. **Tourism** is a significant contributor to national revenues, bringing around US$8.4 billion into the country in 2011. **Fishing**

Visitors who venture out of the major tourist areas should expect to be the subject of gentle curiosity. The often-heard *Dari mana?* and *Mau ke mana?* ('Where are you coming from?'/'Where are you going?') are ritual questions, asked of any stranger. The easiest answer to either question is the equally ritual *Jalan-jalan* ('Just strolling around'). You will often be asked *Sudah bisa makan nasi?* ('Can you eat rice?') as many Indonesians have the idea that Westerners live solely on potatoes and bread.

is an important food source. The **mining** of metals is also quite significant, especially nickel, aluminium, copper, iron, tin and silver – and Indonesia is the world's 5th largest producer of coal.

Mismanagement of **forests** means timber reserves are being rapidly exhausted. This shortage has caused illegal logging even in national parks, although the government has clamped down on this in recent years. The government is being pressurized to convert logging forests to oil palm or pulpwood plantations rather than allow the forest to regenerate naturally, and devolution since 2001 of responsibility for managing natural resources to provincial level has resulted in loss of even the tenuous central control formerly held by the government.

The unit of currency is the **Indonesian rupiah (Rp)**; in 2012 the exchange rate was about Rp 12,300 to the Euro, Rp 15,300 to the UK pound.

THE PEOPLE

Indonesia is the world's fourth most populous nation, with around 250 million people. It contains a colourful assortment of cultures, traditions and people, summed up in the country's motto *Bhinneka Tunggal Ika*, meaning 'Unity in Diversity'. There are more than 100 distinct ethnic groups, and in many cases the only obvious similarity between two citizens is an ability to speak Indonesian, the national language; indeed, many people in remote areas are still unfamiliar with it.

To compare a Christian Batak farmer from **North Sumatra** with an animist Asmat carver from the swamps of **Papua** is like looking for similarities between a Moroccan carpet salesman and a Lapp reindeer herder – and the geographical distance between their home territories is roughly the same.

▶ *Opposite: Workers on a cocoa estate in East Java.*
▼ *Below: Savu horsemen in Timor. The horses are small but surprisingly strong.*

There are, however, rough guidelines for the visitor. The people of the western islands – Java, Bali, Sumatra, and the coastal areas of Kalimantan and Sulawesi – are, in the main, **Malays**. Slender and small-boned, with straight dark hair, most, with the exception of the Hindu Balinese, are Muslim. Travel east from Lombok or Sulawesi, however, and the influence of Melanesia begins to become evident. By the time the traveller reaches Maluku and Papua, the population is utterly different from that of the western islands, with people who are darker-skinned, taller and more heavily built than the Malays of the west.

As the 19th-century explorer and naturalist **Alfred Russel Wallace** noted, the differences between the peoples of Indonesia are not just physical. In his classic book *The Malay Archipelago* (1869) he described a visit to the Kei Islands in the Moluccas:

> I now had my first view of Papuans in their own country … had I been blind I could have been certain these islanders were not Malays. The loud, rapid, eager tones … the intense vital activity manifested in speech and action are the very antipodes of the quiet, unimpulsive Malay. Schoolboys on an unexpected holiday would give but faint idea of the exuberant enjoyment of these people.

Key players in the mosaic of Indonesian peoples are the **Chinese**. Immensely successful in business – from small shops to huge trading conglomerates – they can be compared with the Jews of pre-war Central Europe and, like the Jews, have suffered periodic discrimination and violence. Until liberalization of the media after the end of the Suharto regime, for instance, publications in the Chinese script were banned and people of Chinese descent could not hold public office.

▲ *Above: A traditionally dressed warrior on Nias Island looks anything but warlike – although this could soon change.*

Nowadays the once clear-cut differences between the peoples of the various islands are being eroded as the government works to build a national identity and as people travel increasingly around their country for work and leisure. A standardized education system, television, inter-marriage between different ethnic groups and **migration** (both government-sponsored and spontaneous) between overcrowded Java and Bali to less populated islands have all played their part. Children increasingly learn Indonesian as their first language rather than their regional or tribal tongue, to the extent that scholars worry about the loss even of formerly prominent languages such as Sundanese, the language of western Java, and of the niceties of classical Javanese.

Tribal Groups

Primitive aboriginal tribes, the original settlers of the archipelago, survive in remote forested areas. Semi-nomadic hunter-gatherers, they include the **Kubu** and **Sakhai** of Sumatra and the **Wana** of Central Sulawesi. Most of these groups are now threatened with the loss of their hunting grounds through deforestation and transmigration projects.

Proto-Malay settlers came to the archipelago at least 3000 years ago, retreating inland and to the highlands when later waves of Malay settlers arrived. Major proto-Malay tribes include the **Batak** of North Sumatra, the **Torajans** of the central Sulawesi highlands and the **Dayaks** of Kalimantan. The Dayaks are found mainly in the east and centre, some still living deep in the interior in longhouses along major rivers.

Papua is home to scores of distinctive tribal groups. Darker-skinned, more heavily built and generally with tightly curled hair, the Papuans include the **Dani** of the highlands around the Baliem

Valley, who became known to the outside world only in the late 1930s, and the **Asmat**, wood-carvers living in the swampy plains of the southern coast.

Bajau Laut, or sea gypsies, are found all over eastern Indonesia, living on boats or in stilted settlements on the seashore. Bajau Laut people traditionally did everything at sea in their boats – including giving birth.

Religion

Almost all the great religions are represented among Indonesia's myriad peoples and islands, the nation's diversity extending from this world to the next. With the largest population of **Muslims** of any country, Indonesia is also the most easterly stronghold of **Hinduism** and home to the world's greatest Buddhist monument (Borobudur – *see* page 64) and some of the oldest **Christian** churches in Southeast Asia.

The importance of religion in Indonesia cannot be overestimated. Belief in one supreme God is the first statement of **Pancasila**, the five moral principles which form the core philosophy of modern government in Indonesia, and is part of the glue that holds together – if loosely – a nation of enormously disparate people. Catholicism, Protestantism, Islam, Buddhism and Hinduism are all recognized equally by the government.

As practised in Indonesia, the religions have their own national flavour. Here, perhaps more than anywhere else in the world, religions born of other nations have been accepted and reconciled with animist beliefs which date back to the earliest days of humankind. In **Java** devout Muslims make offerings to **Nyai Loro Kidul**, Goddess of the Southern Seas, and the stories of the Hindu epic *Ramayana* are as well known as the *suras* (chapters) of the Koran. In **Sulawesi** and **Sumba**, Christian villagers stage lavish feasts and sacrifices to send their dead into the afterworld with appropriate honour. Even the Hindus of **Bali** have adapted their religion to encompass more ancient beliefs.

THE MUEZZIN'S CALL

In Indonesia, as in any Muslim nation, believers are expected to pray five times daily. Not all do, of course, but the Imams do their best to call people to pray – including at around 4 in the morning – aided by increasingly powerful speakers. When booking accommodation, you might want to first check the location of the nearest mosque.

◄ *Opposite bottom: Workers in one of the rice paddies of West Java carry out their labours just as countless generations have done before them.*
▼ *Below: The 16th-century Masjid Agung Mosque at Banten. The architecture shows both Islamic and Hindu influences.*

INTRODUCING INDONESIA

MISSIONARIES

Christian missionaries continue to be active in remote areas, notably in Central Sulawesi, Kalimantan and Papua. The flights operated by the Missionary Aviation Fellowship (MAF) are often the only way to reach truly remote settlements. Many of the missionaries are Americans, Europeans or Australians, although growing numbers are Indonesians.

YOUR RELIGIOUS VIEWS

If you fall into conversation with local people you're likely to be asked your religion. Don't mutter about agnosticism or atheism: such viewpoints are incomprehensible in a nation where until very recently identity cards had to carry the bearer's religion. If you are not a member of any of the major religions, it is best to pretend that you are.

▼ Below: A Roman Catholic shrine on Kei Kecil.

The dominant religion, **Islam**, is becoming closer to the orthodox model of the Middle East in many parts of Indonesia. On a day-to-day level, female clothing is now far more conservative than it was two decades ago, with the majority of women in western Indonesia now covering their hair in public.

Another major Indonesian religion is **Balinese Hinduism**, aspects of which might not be recognized by the Hindus of India. It was to Bali that the priests and nobles of Java's Hindu empires fled in the 16th and 17th centuries from an ascendant Islamic state; meanwhile groups of the peasantry retreated to the mountains of eastern Java, where pockets of Hinduism still survive.

Christianity is mainly concentrated in the more remote corners of the archipelago, although there is a significant Christian presence in Java. Some strongly Christian areas – the Batak area of north Sumatra, Ambon, Flores and the Minahasa region of North Sulawesi – were converted by early colonial venturers. The interior of Kalimantan and Papua and the mountains of Tanah Toraja were too inaccessible or too dangerous to penetrate until well into the 20th century, but from the 1930s onwards missionaries have been active in these regions too.

Religion by Regions

Sumatra is predominantly Muslim, with Aceh the most strongly Islamic province. Most of the Batak people of the Lake Toba region, however, are Christian. The Dayak tribes of northern and eastern **Kalimantan** are generally Christian, while coastal dwellers here are descended from Buginese and are mainly Muslim.

Java is almost entirely Muslim, at least nominally: many Javanese have strong beliefs in spirits and practise a form of meditative spiritualism; pre-Islamic beliefs remain strongest in eastern Java. Influential Javanese are trying to foster traditional Javanese beliefs as a way of countering the influence of strict Islamic preachers. The reticent Badui of West Java practise animism, while the Tenggerese around Mt Bromo are Hindus, the last practitioners of a religion which once dominated the island.

Bali is Hindu, although with pockets of Islam in coastal villages and increasingly inland, as Javanese settlers gain a stronger foothold. There is resistance here to the building of mosques with their attendant loud calls to prayer. **Lombok** is mainly Muslim, with a small population of Hindus of Balinese descent. The southern part of **Sulawesi** is a stronghold of Islam, while the Torajan highlanders of the centre are Christians. The Minahasa of North Sulawesi are generally Christian.

▲ *Above: Balinese women and children taking votive offerings to their temple.*

Northern **Maluku**, notably Ternate and Tidore, are Muslim; the southern islands are Christian and Muslim. The Lesser Sundas (Nusa Tenggara) have strongholds of both Islam (Sumbawa) and Christianity (Flores and Sumba). In **Papua** most of the tribes of the interior are now nominally Christian after years of proselytizing by missionaries, although coastal towns are mainly Muslim due to trading influences.

Ramadan

Ramadan, the fasting month, is integral to Islam in Indonesia as elsewhere in the Muslim world. From dawn to dusk, Muslims may not drink, eat or smoke. During this time, restaurants in rural or orthodox Muslim areas are likely to be closed. Visitors should behave with sensitivity – eating or smoking in the street, for instance, is not advised. Events such as dance and theatre performances may be cancelled.

Ramadan culminates in the great Idul Fitri or Lebaran celebrations, a time of hospitality and visiting, when it can seem as if every Muslim in Indonesia is on the move. It is best to try and avoid traveling at this time, as all forms of transport are extremely crowded, seats on planes and trains are hard to obtain, and prices are steeper than normal. The Islamic calendar depends on the phases of the moon and Ramadan moves forward by 10–11 days each year: in 2013 the first day of Ramadan falls on 9 July.

AT THE MOSQUE

Visitors are generally welcome in Indonesia's many mosques, or *mesjid*. Dress with respect and cover your head if you are a woman.

WOMEN'S ROLE IN SOCIETY

Women in Indonesia enjoy greater freedom than in almost any other Muslim nation. Even in heavily Islamic areas like Aceh there is no tradition of purdah, although an increasing number of women cover their hair with a scarf and wear long-sleeved clothing. Segregation of the sexes is confined to the mosque, and one of the country's most important national holidays, Kartini Day, honours an early Javanese campaigner for women's rights.

Found throughout Borneo, longhouses were – and are – uniquely suited to the local climate and culture. Raised high off the ground for ventilation and, in the past, for defence, these structures can be well over 100m (110yd) long and home to dozens of families. Within the building each family has its own apartment, with areas for cooking, sleeping and eating. Outside, a long, covered veranda, often beautifully painted and carved, provides a communal area where rice is pounded, children play and the elderly sit and watch the world go by, protected from rain and sun. The buildings are often fronted by totem poles, 6m (20ft) or more high and carved with fierce warrior figures designed to scare away evil spirits. Some figures boast massive erect phalluses, as jungle spirits apparently do not like sexual arousal.

Staying in a longhouse is an unforgettable experience, but sleep is hard to come by. Pigs and chickens root around underneath, rice is pounded before daybreak, children shriek and hunting dogs howl. The din is astonishing.

ARTS AND CULTURE

One reason for Indonesia's variety of artforms is the country's position at the crossroads of Asia and Melanesia. From Asia come the traditions of Hinduism and Buddhism with their attendant imagery, often superimposed upon a much older tradition of art and religion springing from animist beliefs. The fierce carvings of the Asmat of Papua and the intricate totems of the Dayak of Kalimantan represent the complicated relationships between spirits and nature, with shapes often heavily stylized into a symbolic form of cloud or tree or god, and representations of the cosmic division into upper world and lower world.

With such great distances between different islands and their peoples, cultural unity could hardly be expected. Indeed, such is the difficult terrain in some parts of Indonesia that fascinating differences occurred between groups living just kilometres apart. Until at least the 1930s, for instance, the peoples of Central Sulawesi made cloth from tree-bark because the mountains and thick forests surrounding them were barriers to trade with neighbouring tribes, and woven textiles were unknown. Even now when television, planes, the internet and other forms of communication have helped unify the country, the different ethnic groups retain and develop their unique traditions and arts, and are encouraged to do so by the government.

Textiles

Few visitors to Indonesia leave without buying a locally made textile, whether clothing, tablecloths, pictures or just a length of material. Central Java is particularly well known for its **batik**, produced by stamping or drawing patterns in wax on fine cotton and then dyeing the cloth. The Lesser Sundas, particularly Sumba, are where Indonesia's other internationally known textile technique – *ikat* – originates. *Ikat* means 'tie', and the threads are wound onto a frame and tie-dyed before being woven on a backstrap loom. Although the vegetable dyes used in the past for most textiles are now rare, the original earthy colours of dull red, blue and brown are still popular.

Performing Arts

Throughout Indonesia the important life-stages, especially marriage and death, are celebrated in music, song and dance. Most islands of western and central Indonesia have bronze gongs, bamboo flutes and simple stringed instruments. The most sophisticated orchestras are in Java and Bali, where groups of up to 30 players combine the percussive sounds of metallophones, drums and gongs with one or two flutes, stringed instruments and the human voice. The whole melodic ensemble is known as the *gamelan*.

▲ *Above: Striking traditional Balinese wood carvings on sale in the street.*

The *gamelan* forms the musical backdrop to performances of **dance** or **puppetry**, generally re-enacting the stories of Hindu mythology. The music, dance and drama of Bali are perhaps the most attractive to the casual visitor because of their vitality, glittering colours and dynamic rhythms, while in Central Java the grace of the court dancers and the incredible skill of the master puppeteer manipulating his shadow puppets should not be missed. Indeed, the interest of tourists is helping to maintain these art forms.

Carving and Metalwork

Carving in wood or stone and working metals like bronze, silver and gold are centuries-old crafts known throughout the archipelago. Examples of neolithic stone-working can be seen in the tombs of the Lesser Sundas or the statues of Central Sulawesi, while the fanciful carvings still made for Balinese temples echo the reliefs on the thousand-year-old temples of Java. The techniques of wood carvings stretch from the coastal swamps of Papua to the mountains of Sumatra, where villagers decorate their clan houses with carved and coloured panels.

At celebrations Indonesians bedeck themselves in particular finery. Examples of the colourful beadwork of Kalimantan can be seen in museums or handicraft shops in Jakarta, and most provincial museums hold fine gold or silver regalia. The silver ornaments of Yogyakarta, still beautifully crafted using ancient tech-

TOURIST PERFORMANCES

Don't miss the skilful performances of dance, music and puppetry put on for tourists. Indonesians are justifiably proud of their culture and mostly present it to a very high standard. The performances are shortened for Western tastes, but are none the worse for this. Not many tourists are prepared to sit through a traditional all-night performance of Javanese shadow-puppetry – and in fact Indonesians themselves are now much less likely to do so, so that moves are afoot to re-package performances for the domestic market too.

Indonesia's craftsmen and merchants have long realized that overseas visitors will pay top prices for antiques. Entire villages busily turn them out – such as Mojokerto in East Java, where wonderful replicas of 13th-century Majapahit crafts are produced, including marvellous statues in stone, terracotta – and even gold. Usually 'antiques' are produced to cater to market tastes for old-style ornaments rather than to deceive. Art-lovers seeking to buy genuine Asmat carvings should be careful – large numbers of fake pieces are produced in Java or Bali. In 1993 Asmat carvers tried to take legal action against one Javanese village for breach of copyright!

▼ *Below: A Javanese market offers all sorts of exotic delicacies for the jaded palate.*

niques, make excellent souvenirs – easier to carry home than a full-size bronze gong!

Crafts and Shopping

Indonesia's long history and its range of cultures come to dazzling life in the teeming markets and fascinating craft villages. Many traditional crafts are deeply rooted in the culture of their island of origin. To appreciate them to the full, it is most rewarding to buy from the region where they are produced rather than from a souvenir shop in Java or Bali – although for people without the time to visit remote regions of the country, the government-sponsored handicraft stores have excellent examples from all over the archipelago at reasonable prices. The simplest craft items are found in the markets: a woven basket for winnowing rice, a bamboo flute, a long-handled rice spoon or a plain earthenware bowl.

Bargaining

If a shop has price tags on its goods it's likely to be a *harga pas*, or fixed-price establishment, as with the majority of department stores. If there are no price tags, prepare to bargain – for everything from earrings to a four-poster bed (it's worth trying this even if there is a price-tag). Where possible, try to establish in advance a reasonable price for the item you hope to buy – your hotel may help. Otherwise consult fixed-price establishments or government-run craft centres for a guide price. Bear in mind that hotel shops tend to be very expensive, and if prices are quoted in US dollars they will be higher than the rupiah price.

If interested in an item, casually ask about it. The trader will normally quote a price. Look horrified and reel backwards muttering *Mahal, mahal!* ('Expensive, expensive!'). Come back with an offer perhaps 30% of the trader's price, and then settle down to business. Beware of 'over-bargaining', i.e. driving the price down too far – sometimes, especially towards the end of the day, small traders will settle for a low sum just to have enough cash to buy food.

Where to Buy It

Java

Jakarta is strong on clothes, furniture and 'antiques' – in Indonesian, the word 'antik' simply means that something is made in an old-fashioned style. **Yogyakarta** has carvings, silver, leatherwork, batik and *wayang* puppets. **Solo** has puppets, batik, carving and pottery.

▲ Above: A Balinese handicrafts shop.

Sumatra

Medan has a good range of crafts (lots of Batak items), including some imports from Kalimantan. **Padang** has palm-leaf basketry and weaving. You might find beautiful, simple wooden bowls and dishes from Siberut. **Kota Gedang (Bukittinggi)** has filigree silver.

Kalimantan

Samarinda is good for antique Chinese ceramics, fantastic Dayak carvings and crafts, and beautiful silk sarongs. **Banjarmasin** is best for precious and semi-precious stones, with a great range of stones, from garnets to diamonds.

Bali

One of the craft and fashion capitals of Southeast Asia, making the latest designer clothing, silverware, carvings (wood and stone), paintings, masks and more. **Kuta** is Fashion City – arrive in a T-shirt and leave with a complete wardrobe. Many European designers work from Bali and their designs appear in Kuta shops a season before they arrive in the West.

Lombok

Most of the same crafts as Bali, but with the addition of some attractive heavy pottery and wonderful weaving (sensational curtaining and upholstery material).

Sulawesi

Makassar is good for silver and gold filigree jewellery and brightly coloured silks. **Rantepao** stocks bead jewellery and wall-hangings, carved wooden panels and ebony-handled knives.

CREATIVE BARGAINING

Bargaining can take some time, with each side modifying the price by degrees. Treat it as fun, and hope to conclude a deal at not more than half the first price – experts will go for one-third, but for that you need time on your hands. Be sure you really want the item before you start bargaining – it is bad manners to reach a mutually agreeable price and then not buy. If bargaining gets sticky, try walking out – if the owner stops you, a deal has been made. But don't lose a lovely piece of jewellery or weaving for the sake of a few rupiah.

Some of the best **coffee** in the world is grown in the highlands of Sumatra and Java, and good **tea** is also produced. Both tea and coffee are drunk without milk and very sweet; if you don't want sugar added to your tea or coffee, tell the waiter you want it served *pahit* (bitter). Outside major hotels don't expect real **milk** if you ask for it with your coffee or tea: it will usually be sweetened condensed milk.

Nusa Tenggara

Most of the Lesser Sundas produce unique woven fabrics.

Food and Drink

Indonesian food, especially in Java and Sumatra, can be rather spicy to unaccustomed Western palates; the hottest of all comes from the **Padang region** of West Sumatra, served in restaurants all over the archipelago. In general, the further east you travel the less spicy the food, but beware of lurking chilli peppers everywhere. If you are caught, don't reach for water: plain boiled rice, a slice of cucumber or a banana is much more effective.

Rice is the essential food throughout most of Indonesia: eaten boiled or fried and in enormous quantities, it takes the place of both bread and potatoes. Moving east into Maluku and Papua, **cassava**, **sweet potatoes** and **sago** take over as staples, although rice is generally still available.

For most Indonesians **meat** is rather expensive and is usually eaten only in small quantities. Typically, a meal might consist of two or more vegetables and a fish, meat or chicken dish, together with a hot chilli sauce (*sambal*) or pickled vegetables. Chicken and goat are common foods all over the archipelago. For obvious reasons, pork is rarely found in Muslim areas except in Chinese restaurants. **Fish**, eaten fresh or dried, is the major source of protein for tens of millions of Indonesians.

Many Javanese dishes contain tofu (*tahu*) or *tempeh*, a delicious nutty 'cake' made from soya beans – perfect for vegetarians.

Coconut oil and **coconut milk** are used in curries and many sauces, along with lemon grass, ginger, cumin,

▼ *Below: This village market in Bali could hardly be more traditional.*

turmeric, coriander and galangal. In Sumatra and Java, especially, tiny **dried fish** and **chilli peppers** are pounded into a paste and added to dishes to intensify the flavours.

Although each region has its own specialities, some dishes extend across the archipelago. **Fried rice** and **fried noodles** (*nasi goreng* and *mie goreng*) are found everywhere. Originally from Java, *gado gado* – a cooked vegetable salad in a peanut sauce – is also widely available. Chicken or goat *satay*, barbecued over a charcoal brazier and served with a peanut sauce, can be bought on almost every street corner.

▲ *Above: Luscious – and, most important, cooling – fresh fruit on sale in the streets of Jakarta.*

Regional specialities abound – although not all might appeal. A Batak speciality from North Sumatra is the part-digested cud of water buffalo, while the Minahasa of North Sulawesi enjoy the meat of dog, fruit bat and rat. Throughout Maluku and Papua sago grubs are a prized delicacy, while Balinese children enjoy roasted dragonfly.

Elsewhere the exoticism is more acceptable to Western palates. In Tanah Toraja try buffalo meat baked in bamboo tubes, or roast suckling pig in Bali. In Samarinda, East Kalimantan, ask for the huge prawns. For a real taste of Indonesia, try eating at one of the food stalls (*warung*) which spring up at dusk in every town and city – if you stick to freshly cooked food, tummy upsets are unlikely.

If for no other reason, it is worth visiting Indonesia to sample the **fruit**. Bananas come in dozens of varieties, while mango, papaya and pineapple taste quite different when they have ripened naturally. Don't miss the hairy red rambutan, or the mangosteen, with its luscious melting flesh inside a hard burgundy shell. Most infamous is the huge, thorny **durian**, banned from planes and hotels because of its pervasive and unmistakable smell. It 'does something' for human aficionados, along with other mammals – elephants love it, and forest workers know not to keep it in camp because it attracts tigers. The creamy flesh tastes like a buttery egg custard with hints of a rich Madeira, cream cheese, liver pâté … and more. Be warned – you risk becoming an addict!

COLD DRINKS

Alcohol is usually available in the form of beer. In the main cities and tourist centres you will also find spirits, but the Indonesian-made ones are dire. Australian wines are available in Bali and Jakarta. **Ice** is made in government-controlled factories from purified water and rarely causes illness. Drink only freshly boiled or bottled **water** – the many brands widely available are all known as *Aqua*. For a really thirst-quenching drink, try young **coconut juice** straight from the coconut (*jus kelapa muda*). Add some rum for a tropical cocktail.

2
Sumatra

The fifth-largest island in the world, Sumatra spans more than 1700km (1050 miles) from northwest to southeast, and accounts for a quarter of Indonesia's total landmass. It is an island of dense forests, extensive mangrove swamps and towering volcanoes, of fascinating cultures, wonderful wildlife and cosmopolitan cities.

The most popular destination is the vast **Lake Toba** in North Sumatra, homeland of the Batak people. To the west are the **Nias Islands**, with their astonishing stone megaliths, sandy beaches and massive longhouses. Further south are the **Minangkabau Highlands**, where the Minang, a matriarchal group who are also devout Muslims, live in some of the loveliest traditional houses in Indonesia.

Sumatra is justly famous, too, for its wildlife, now protected in national parks like **Gunung Leuser, Kerinci Seblat** and **Way Kambas**. Indigenous animals include orang-utan, elephant, rhinoceros, tiger and the Sumatran crocodile. In the forests huge trees festooned with vines and epiphytes rise 30m (100ft) or more from the forest floor, and in the mountains running parallel to the west coast it is possible to see the parasitic rafflesia, the largest flower in the world.

Although Sumatra's cities are rapidly expanding and industrializing, most of this vast island remains an adventure to visit, with many people still living traditional lifestyles based on agriculture and even hunter-gathering. Most Sumatrans are Muslims, although the Bataks of Lake Toba and Berastagi and most Nias Islanders are Christians.

CLIMATE

Sumatra straddles the Equator, and the monsoon period in the north differs from that in the south. In the north the rainiest time is from Oct until Mar or Apr, and the dry season runs May–Sep. In the south the monsoon period also starts in Oct, but in Dec–Feb the rains are truly torrential. The best time to visit is towards the end of the dry season. In recent years the skies have been clogged in the dry season with haze generated by illegal fires used to clear the forest.

◄ *Opposite: A fisherman's seasonal dwelling.*

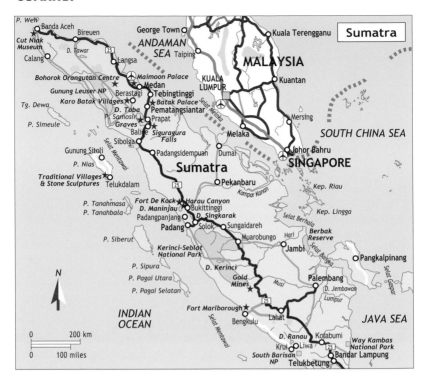

DON'T MISS

*** Samosir Island: the Toba Batak here have traditional villages with splendid tombs and megaliths.

** Tangkahan Elephant Trekking: the best way to see the rainforest, from the backs of well-cared-for elephants.

** Kerinci Seblat National Park: dominated by an active volcano and with the beautiful Lake Kerinci.

* Bohorok Orang-utan Centre: see the great apes at close quarters.

ACEH

Banda Aceh

With much renovation after the 2004 tsunami, Banda Aceh is a staunchly Islamic town with a fine mosque. There are monuments dedicated to victims of the tsunami, and some extraordinary sights such as a boat washed inland sitting atop a house. Most tourists arrive here en route to Pulau Weh (Weh Island).

PULAU WEH

This is Indonesia's most northerly (and westerly) point. The atmosphere here is relaxed, with excellent beach tourism and diving. Head for the main town of Sabang, then to beaches and smaller islands.

NORTH SUMATRA
Medan

First-time visitors to Indonesia who arrive in Medan should prepare themselves for the fourth largest city in Indonesia, a noisy industrial giant. As an important regional hub for trade throughout Sumatra and the Malay peninsula, it has several buildings reflecting the wealth of both colonial and post-independence times. Maimoon Palace, built in 1886, was the home of the Sultanate of Deli, and the nearby Grand Mosque (1906) is attractive. The Central Post Office and the Harrison & Crosfield building are fine examples of Dutch architecture.

Medan has the largest Indian quarter of any Indonesian city (Kampung Keling), with a Hindu temple ornamented in riotous colour, built in 1884. It also has a large Chinese population, and the Taoist temple, also intricately decorated, is the largest in Sumatra. The North Sumatra Museum has replicas of traditional Batak houses and a good display of tribal artefacts. The Zoo is worth a look, and can be combined with a visit to the crocodile farm – Indonesia's largest – at **Pam Sunggal**.

The city is the main departure point for tours of northern Sumatra. The scenery becomes increasingly beautiful as you climb into the hills.

Lake Toba and the Toba Batak ✶✶

Around 3 hours from Medan and the same from Brastagi lie **Lake Toba** and **Samosir Island**, heartland of the Batak people. Like the Torajanese of Sulawesi and the Minangkabau of West Sumatra, the Bataks are proto-Malays, descendants of some of the earliest settlers of the Indonesian archipelago. They were once feared for their fierceness and their practice of ritual cannibalism. Today, although churches are packed on Sundays, animism and ancestor veneration survive.

Toba is the largest freshwater lake in Southeast Asia and, at 505m (1657ft) deep, one of the deepest in the world. It was formed by a monumental volcanic eruption around 74,000 years ago. Water levels fell in the 1980s when the **Asahan River** was dammed for hydroelectricity.

The direct route to Lake Toba leads south from Medan, parallel to the coast, before turning inland for the long

▲ *Above: Orang-utan mother and infant at the Bohorok Orang-utan Centre.*

▼ *Below: Water levels in Lake Toba have fallen in recent years, but it still retains its beauty.*

climb into the hills around the lake. En route, stop in **Pematangsiantar** for a visit to the **Simalungun Museum** or detour to the fortified village of **Pematang Purba**, where several tribal longhouses are preserved.

Be sure to see a sigale-gale puppet dance performance. These lifesize puppets were traditionally used to revive the souls of the dead, which then possessed the puppets and communicated with the living.

Bohorok Orang-utan Centre *

Just 2 hours from Medan, the Bohorok Orang-utan Centre offers a virtually guaranteed sighting of young and mature orang-utans. It lies in the jungle 40 minutes' walk along a good path from the village of Bukit Lawang. There is still a thriving, although illegal, trade in young orang-utans, and most of the animals here have been rescued from it. The problem in returning the apes to the forest is that most were captured as babies. Staff teach the animals survival skills before their release into remote areas of the Gunung Leuser National Park. After a flash flood in 2003 which destroyed many of the tourist facilities the village has re-emerged as a friendly and laid-back destination with a good range of accommodation. It's a good place for short jungle treks.

Prapat **

Prapat is the main tourist base on the shore of Lake Toba, and is blissfully cool after the heat of Medan. It has wonderful views over the lake, good swimming, a Cultural Centre and a range of pleasant resort hotels. It also has a life apart from tourism: try to catch the Saturday market (near the ferry terminal), where Bataks from outlying villages come to shop, sell or just gossip.

Around Prapat

Balige, an hour or so to the south, has some interesting traditional buildings, good-quality weaving and, nearby, old tombs – many adorned with lifesize statues and carvings. **Labuhan Garaga**, about 30 minutes' drive from Prapat, is another weaving centre; the heavy cotton blankets make excellent cushion covers.

N

Samosir Island ★★★

Homeland of the Toba Batak, Samosir has drawn travellers for decades. The main arrival point is the traditional village of **Tomok**, which boasts the tomb of the pre-Christian Raja Sidabuta, his queen and his mistress. The small museum is worth a look. There is good shopping at stalls selling everything from carvings to musical instruments and magic calendars. The Toba Batak of Samosir are a distinct group and have several special ceremonies, including one held in July to give thanks for blessings, complete with dancing, music, traditional costumes and buffalo slaughter.

If you see no other traditional Batak village, see **Ambarita**. There are three megalithic complexes with stone seats and tables, including the flat stone slab upon which prisoners were killed.

Simanindo has a remarkable raja's palace and ancient fortifications. The 10 sets of buffalo horns on the palace each represent a generation of kings.

Brastagi and the Karo Batak

A cool hill town, Brastagi (or Berastagi) is a good base from which to explore Karo Batak villages, climb volcanoes, buy handicrafts, or sample locally grown *markisa* – passion fruit. Some Karo Batak villagers live in massive clan houses raised off the ground on strong pillars and serving as home to eight or more families. People occasionally still wear dark traditional clothes, the men in heavy black turbans and the women with broad, tasselled headdresses and huge silver earrings.

Around Brastagi

Lingga has about 30 ornately decorated clan houses. **Barusjahe** is similar to Lingga but less visited and friendlier. Ask to see the *geriten*, small replica houses, where bones of dead Karo nobles were stored. Nearby is the village of Peceran, with some beautifully preserved old houses. **Cingkes** (40 minutes by car) has about 20 clan houses and a spirit house. **Sibolangit Botanical Gardens**, between Medan and Brastagi, has paved paths and is a good introduction to tropical vegetation.

EATING TIPS

If you don't like your food liberally spiced with chilli peppers, tell your waiter you want food that is *tidak pedas* – 'not spicy hot'. In Padang restaurants, waiters carry many dishes to your table balanced along their arms, and you pay only for what you eat. Many dishes are cooked in the morning and served at room temperature, with rice served hot.

▼ *Below: Rafting through rapids on the Alas River.*

▼ *Below: Known misleadingly as the Cannibal King's Dinner Table, the stone slab in Ambarita on which prisoners were put to death.*

Gunung Leuser National Park **

One of the largest national parks in Asia, Gunung Leuser covers more than 7750km² (3000 sq miles) and protects more than 100 different mammals – including rhinoceros, tiger, elephant and orang-utan – and at least 300 species of bird. The eastern fringes of the park can be visited from Brastagi, but for naturalists and trekkers the best entry point is the town of Kutacane, a half-day drive through the mountains from Brastagi.

Spectacular river-rafting trips are available down the wild Alas River through farmland and virgin rainforest; lasting 2–5 days, the adventure offers probably your best chance to see local wildlife.

Nias Island

Wild and mountainous, riven by dramatic gorges and fast-flowing rivers, Nias is an island where the culture competes with the landscape for attention. Stone staircases rise up steep mountainsides to fortified villages where the chief once sat on a stone throne, carved with writhing snakes, to watch sacrifices made on huge stone altars. In village squares 2m (6ft) high pyramidal structures were used to train young warriors to leap over protective fortifications – the origin of the ritual *fahombe* dance.

Headhunting ceased long ago and, since the arrival of Protestant missionaries, the art of megalith-building has been lost. The villages remain, however, as do the stone altars and megaliths. The island suffered considerable damage in the 2004 tsunami and a major earthquake a few months later. Facilities were rebuilt with the help of aid agencies.

Around Nias

Most visitors stay in beautiful **Lagundri Bay**, a beautiful horseshoe-shaped bay in the south of the island, famous for its world-class surfing, or in the small port of **Telukdalam**. The airport (served by flights from Padang and Medan) is in the north of the island at **Gunung Sitoli**.

Bawomataluwo (20min from Telukdalam) is a picture-postcard village with a huge royal palace built on piles – each one an entire treetrunk. Inside the palace are amazing carvings; the village square has further carvings and almost 300 megaliths. Down the hill (take the stone steps) is the village of **Orahili**.

At **Hilisimaetano** around 140 traditional houses survive, as do many megaliths; stone-jumping takes place most Saturdays. **Hilimaeta**, near Lagundri (a 40min walk), has monuments including stone tables and chairs and a 2m (6ft) stone penis. Walk up to the village by a stone staircase.

WEST SUMATRA
Padang

The capital of West Sumatra province, Padang is a prosperous city and major port. It was badly damaged in an earthquake in 2009, but the resilient West Sumatrans are rebuilding their city. **Adityawarman Museum** (closed on Mondays) is built in traditional Minang style, with rice barns at the front. Its collections were badly damaged in the earthquake. **Taman Budaya** (opposite the museum) is an arts institute which often stages Minang dance and *pencak silat* (martial arts) performances. Chinese temples by the small harbour, **Muara**, are symphonies of colour in red lacquer and gold leaf. **Air Manis**, a fishing village beyond Muara, is worth the 40min walk, which takes you past old Japanese cannon and a Chinese cemetery.

Around and from Padang

Cubadak Island, with the Paradiso Village resort, is one of Indonesia's newest getaways – an hour and a half from Padang by road plus 10 minutes by boat. The **Solok** area, up in the mountains, is famous for its many Minang houses, rice and traditional clothes – including women's headdresses like Viking helmets consisting of lengths of folded cloth.

If you drive to Bukittinggi, take the long route via Solok, **Lake Singkarak** and **Sulit Air** (many ravishing traditional houses). Just south of **Pariaman** a Tabuik Festival is held annually – the date varies according to the Muslim calendar. Villagers build and decorate *bouraq* – winged horses with the face of a woman – which are paraded through the streets, with mock fights whenever two *bouraq* cross paths.

Independence Day (Aug 17) celebrations in **Palembang** include the **Bidar Race** on the Musi River; long, narrow canoes shaped like animals powered by up to 50 oarsmen. The city's **Rumah Bari Museum** has mesolithic sculptures from the Pasemah Highlands and a 200-year-old royal barge. **Candi Muara Takus** is a Buddhist stupa complex thought to date from the 9th century. **Siak Palace**, 2 hours from Pekanbaru, is an amazing Moorish-style building (built in 1889), all columns and chandeliers. There are more ancient temple remains at the Muara Jambi complex an hour's drive or boat trip from the city.

▼ *Below: Near Bukittinggi, a village on the shore of Maninjau crater lake.*

SUMATRA

THE MINANGKABAU

The name Minangkabau means 'victorious buffalo'. According to legend, rather than stage a potentially catastrophic battle with an invading Javanese army, it was decided to settle the issue by means of a bullfight. The Javanese imported the largest, fiercest bull they could find. The Minang found a young calf and starved it for days. The Javanese rocked with laughter – but the Minang had the last laugh. They tied sharp spikes to the calf's head and the starving creature gored the Javanese bull to death in a desperate search for milk.

▼ *Below: A coconut collector in West Sumatra: the macaque climbs the trees for him.*

Minangkabau Highlands

High above the steaming coastal heat of Padang lies **Bukittinggi**, capital of the Minangkabau people. This area draws thousands of visitors every year, with foreign tourists increasingly joined by tourists from Java exploring their own country. The attraction is the beautiful mountain scenery combined with a fascinating culture and pleasant climate. Anthropologists, too, continue to be drawn to the Minangkabau Highlands by a culture which is both Muslim and matriarchal.

Bukittinggi

The name means 'high hill', and the town is stunningly located with views over fertile valleys to two volcanoes, **Mt Merapi** and **Mt Singgalang**. Climbing Merapi to see the dawn from the summit is a popular and spectacular trip. Although it has not erupted seriously since the 1980s, puffs of smoke and occasionally small ash explosions can be seen from across the valley, and it is best to check locally if the mountain is considered safe.

The town itself is clean, relaxed and prosperous. It is a tradition for young men to journey to other parts of Indonesia to seek their fortune before returning home to get married, and the Minang are respected across Indonesia for their sharp business sense. Bukittinggi is laid out in tiers down the steep hillside, each level connected to the next by precipitous stone steps and passageways.

Your first port of call should be the aptly named **Panorama Park**, which has spectacular views over the Sianok and Ngarai canyons. Stairs take you down to the valley bottom for the two-hour walk to the silversmithing centre of **Koto Gedang**.

Below the town square, with its old Dutch clock tower, is a colourful market that draws villagers from far around, with stalls selling everything from chilli peppers to love potions. Bukittinggi's zoo offers a chance to see many different animals and birds in a beautiful parkland setting. Below the zoo are caves excavated by the Japanese during World War II and now a tourist attraction. Far more spectacular – although further afield (25 minutes by car) – is the **Ngalau Kamang cave complex**, with its spectacular stalactites and stalagmites.

From Bukittinggi

A 30min drive through rich river valleys with multidomed mosques and tantalizing glimpses of traditional Minang houses takes you to **Padangpanjang**, famous for its rain, its cold nights and its college of traditional Indonesian arts, STSI. Live performances of traditional Minangkabau dance and music, as well as *gamelan*, feature during term-times. These dates are extremely flexible – each institution across Indonesia seems to have different ones – and the dates vary from year to year. Ask for information about performances at the tourist office.

Some 40 minutes west of Bukittinggi, through lush, rolling hills, lies the huge and beautiful crater lake of **Maninjau**. Walk down from the top of the hill (about an hour) to enjoy the peace and the views.

At **Batusankar** you can see the splendidly restored palace, with its wonderful carved and painted façades. Even at weekends, when there are crowds, it is intensely atmospheric. **Balimbing** village has many traditional Minang homes.

Harau Canyon, near Payakumbuh, is a deep canyon with a beautiful waterfall (best at the end of the rainy season) and many butterflies; avoid weekends, when it becomes very crowded. Steam-train buffs must see **Padangpanjang Station**, where relics rust stylishly in sidings. Giant rafflesia flowers are sometimes found at a sanctuary at **Batang Palapuh**, near Lake Maninjau.

BULLFIGHTS

Bullfights are held regularly in villages around Bukittinggi. Two bulls of similar size and weight are set loose to battle for supremacy. The loser is the first to take flight. Fights are held most Saturdays at Kota Baru and Air Agnat.

▼ *Below: Typical Minang-kabau architecture in the splendid setting of the Harau Canyon.*

KERINCI SEBLAT

This national park is one of Asia's most important wildlife areas with more than 350 species of bird and 60 species of mammal – including sun-bears, clouded leopards and golden cats. It is one of the most important areas for **tiger** in the world and part of a 'Cluster World Heritage Site', along with the Gunung Leuser and Bukit Barisan National Parks. **Bird-watchers** usually stay in Kersiktua, at the foot of Mt Kerinci, at Subandi's Homestay where a log of bird records is kept. Trekking opportunities are virtually unlimited to the adventurous although there is little tourist infrastructure.

Kerinci Seblat National Park **

A seven-hour drive from Padang, the 14,000km² (5404-sq-mile) Kerinci Seblat is one of the most important wildlife parks in Southeast Asia. Endangered animals include tapir, the Sumatran tiger, clouded leopard, Sumatran rhinoceros and elephant – but no orang-utans (in Sumatra these occur only north of Lake Toba). Local people and foreign researchers report seeing something even stranger: an ape-like creature known as 'orang pendek' (short person). It hasn't yet been accepted by science, but its existence is thought likely.

The active volcano Mt Kerinci, at 3805m (12,484ft), is the highest mountain in Indonesia outside Papua. Most visitors base themselves in the small market town of **Sungeipenuh**, in the densely populated river valley. The town is a 20min drive from **Lake Kerinci**, which offers beautiful and easy walking to villages around the lakeshore.

The two-hour drive from Sungeipenuh to Mt Kerinci is by a good road and offers superlative views. The climb up the mountain takes two days – be prepared for a cold night camping out on the slopes. At the base of **Mt Tujuh**, near Palompek village below Mt Kerinci, is a National Park forest guesthouse. Climb on via jungle trails to **Lake Tujuh** (three hours), an eerily beautiful crater lake. An hour from the guesthouse is the enormous **Letter W Waterfall**.

Bengkulu

On the shore of the Indian Ocean, Bengkulu was the last territory in Indonesia to be held by the British. The British presence was established in 1685, but the city's fame and prosperity reached its apogee in the early 19th century under Sir Thomas Stamford Raffles, who went on to found Singapore – but lost four of his five children to tropical disease here. Today Bengkulu is a pleasant city with many tree-lined roads and small parks.

Fort Marlborough dates from 1714. Nearby is the **British Governor's mansion**, its classical façade overrun by vines and banyan-tree roots. The **Kuburan Belanda** ('foreigners' graveyard') dates back to the early 18th century. Don't miss the strangely atmospheric house where Sukarno, Indonesia's first presi-

▼ *Below: Mount Kerinci broods over Kerinci Seblat.*

dent, lived during years of exile under the Dutch. **Pantai Panjang** ('Long Beach') stretches for kilometres. Be careful – the surf produces strong undertows.

Around Bengkulu

Tabah Penanjung, an hour into the hills above Bengkulu, is a nature reserve where rafflesia are often found. **Mt Bukit Kaba**, near the pleasant hill town of Curup, can be climbed in a day from Bengkulu if you leave early; the mountain boasts three immense craters and bubbling sulphur fountains. At Seblat, north of Bengkulu, is an elephant conservation centre housing elephants removed from conflicts with farming communities. South of Bengkulu, the coastline is beautiful on the way to the little town of **Krui.** Stay at **Krui** or **Liwa** to explore the Bukit Barisan National Park. Krui is best known as a surfers' destination.

LAMPUNG

At the extreme south of Sumatra, Lampung province is known for its marvellous 'ship cloths', some using real gold thread, and for its pepper. In the 1970s and 80s it was the location for ambitious transmigration projects, resettling farmers from overpopulated Java. It boasts volcanoes, wildlife reserves, megalithic remains, a coastline of deep-cut bays and wonderful beaches – and, thanks to the Javanese settlers, rice-paddy systems to rival those of their ancestral homeland.

The provincial capital is **Bandar Lampung**, made up of the twin cities of Telukbetung and Tanjungkarang. The area was devastated by tsunamis generated by the 1883 eruption of **Krakatau**, and in Telukbetung a ship's buoy lies where it was thrown, halfway up a hill. In Bandar Lampung, visit the provincial museum at Jl Teuku Umar for archaeological exhibits and exquisite antique fabrics.

Way Kambas National Park is a 130,000ha (320,000-acre) area of freshwater swamp and lowland forest with elephants, tigers, tapirs and many other animals, including a good range of birds. The first elephant trainiing centre in Indonesia started here in the mid-1980s, since when it has dealt with some of Sumatra's surplus elephants by domesticating them and sending them to zoos and safari parks.

SUMATRA'S EAST COAST

After the mountains and rain-forests of West Sumatra, the flatness of the east coast is a surprise. This is a land of big skies and oil rigs and nights lit by natural-gas flares: the area is the major source of Indonesia's oil and gas wealth. Giant rivers like the **Musi** and **Siak** snake their way from sources more than 150km (100 miles) inland through mangrove swamps and jungle, past settlements on stilts, to ports like Pekanbaru, midway up the coast, and Palembang, which has historical records going back 13 centuries. The islands of **Batam** and **Bintan** are part of the Southeast Asian 'golden triangle' of economic growth, with industries and tourist resorts, including luxury hotels and golf courses which cater largely to the weekend Singapore market.

SUMATRA AT A GLANCE

GETTING THERE

By air: Major cities in Sumatra have regular flights to Jakarta, Singapore and Malaysia.

By sea: For those with more time to spare, the state shipping company Pelni runs efficient passenger ships linking the main ports (including Medan and Padang). Travel first-class for comfort.

GETTING AROUND

Road travel is no longer the ordeal it was, and roads are improving every year. But do not underestimate the distances that are involved. Cars with drivers and guides are easily organized and available in all the main centres. Make sure you agree in advance exactly what is included. The better-quality buses are fine for short distances.

WHERE TO STAY

The main centres – Medan, Banda Aceh, Padang, Bukittinggi, Brastagi, Lake Toba, etc. – have a good range of international hotels. Elsewhere, be prepared to compromise.

Banda Aceh
LUXURY
Hermes Palace Hotel, Jl Panglima Nyak Makam, tel: 0651 755 5888, www.hermespalacehotel.com

Weh Island
Pulau Weh Resort, www.pulauwehresort.com Good for diving as well as general stays.

Freddie's, Santai Sumur, tel: 0813 6025 5001, www.santai-sabang.com saintaisumurtiga@yahoo.com.au

Medan
LUXURY
Tiara Medan, Jl Cut Mutiah, tel: 061 457 4000, fax: 061 451 0176, www.tiarahotel.com
Aryaduta Hotel Medan, Jl Kapten Maulana Lubis 8, tel: 021 385 8770, www.aryaduta.com

MID-RANGE
Hotel Bumi Asih, Jl Sei Bohorok Baru 20, tel: 061 415 6298, fax: 061 415 9198, www.hotelbumiasih.com/medan
Hotel Deli River, Jl Raya Namorambe 129, tel: 061 703 2964, www.hotel-deliriver.com Located just outside Medan in a tranquil riverside location.
Soechi International Hotel, Jl Cirebon 76a, tel: 061 456 1234, www.soechi-hotel.com

Brastagi
Most popular up-market hotel here is the **Grand Mutiara,** Jl Peceran, tel: 0628 91555, www.grandmutiarahotel.com

Prapat
Dozens of hotels and guesthouses to choose from, although weekends can get busy. Among the nicest are:
Inna Parapat, Jl Marihat 1.
Danau Toba Internasional, Jl Pulau Samosir 17, tel: 0625 41583, fax: 0625 41119.

Samosir Island
Most of the accommodation on Samosir is simple, although some more comfortable hotels have been developed. The main places to stay are Tuk Tuk and Ambarita.

There are dozens of hotels and guesthouses. Try **Hotel Carolina Cottages**, tel: 0625 451 210, www.carolina-cottages.com Alternatives are the **Toledo Inn**, tel: 0625 41429, and the more up-market **Tabo Cottages**, tel: 0625 451 318, www.tabocottages.com
Barbara's, tel: 0625 41230, has a well-established reputation for friendliness, while the **Sopo Toba**, tel: 0625 700 0009, www.hotelsopotoba.com More of a traditional resort hotel, and one of the most up-market on the island.

Nias
There are several basic guesthouses around Lagundri Bay and Sorake Beach aimed at backpackers and surfers, with facilities to match. Visit www.sorakebeach.org for the latest information.

Padang
Villa Air Manis, Jl Air Manis 88, Bukit Gado Gado, Padang, tel: 0751 767 888, www.airmanis.com
Pangeran Beach Hotel, Jl Ir H. Juanda 79, tel: 0751 31333, fax: 0751 54613.
Ambacang Hotel, Jl Bundo Kanduang 14–16, tel: 0751 39888, fax: 0751 39966.

Cubadak Island
Cubadak Paradiso Village, tel. 081 2660 3766, www.cubadak-paradiso village.com

Bukittinggi
As this is a popular backpacker destination, there are many guesthouses at the lower end of the market, followed by more up-market hotels such as:
Pusako, Jl Soekarno-Hatta 7, tel: 0752 32111, www.pusako hotel.com
Hills Hotel, Jl Laras Datuk Bandaro, tel: 0752 35000, www.thehillsbukittinggi.com
Campago Hotel, Jl Cempaka 1, tel. 0752 35151, www. campagoresorthotel.com

Sungaipenuh
Most of the hotels in this town are basic. Well above the rest is the **Hotel Mahkota** – simple but clean and quiet; Jl Depati Parbo, tel: 0748 21640. For bird-watchers, the best place to stay is **Pak Subandi's Homestay** at Kersiktua, tel: 0748 357 009.

Bengkulu
Grage Horison Hotel, Jl Pantai Nala 142, tel: 0736 21722, www.gragehorizon.com
Hotel Splash, Jl Sudirman 48, tel. 0818 0449 4497, www. hotel-splash.com Business hotel.

Bandar Lampung
Most hotels in this area can help visitors to organize trips to Way Kambas (around two hours from the city). These trips generally include boat trips up the Way Kanan River.
Sheraton Lampung Hotel, Jl Wolter Monginsidi, tel. 0721 486 666, www.starwood. hotels.com
Bukit Randu Hotel, Jl Kamboja 1–2, tel: 0721 241 333, www.bukitrandu.com

Palembang
Hotel Horison, Jl Kapten A. Rivai, tel: 0711 355 500, www.horisonpalembang.com
Hotel Duta, Jl Letkol Iskandar 535, tel: 0711 373 800, fax: 0711 372 951, www.hotel dutapalembang.com

Pekanbaru
Sri Indrayani, Jl Dr Sam Ratulangi, tel: 0761 35600, fax: 0761 31870.
Mutiara Merdeka, Jl Yos Sudarso 12, tel: 0761 31272, www.mutiara-merdeka.com

SHOPPING
Excellent coffee can be had all over Sumatra, often straight from the plantations where it's grown. Drink it locally – then buy some to take home as a souvenir. And rather than the international chains of coffee shops, try the coffee in the Indonesian-owned J.Co outlets.

Medan
Jl Achmad Yani, the city's main shopping street for souvenirs, has dozens of shops selling Batak carvings, fabrics and other tribal artefacts. The huge **Medan Mall** has clothing shops and good food outlets.

Padang
For souvenirs and artefacts Bukittinggi is probably better, but the **Matahari Shopping Centre** (Jl Moh Yamin) has clothing and basic necessities, while **Sartika** (Jl Sudirman 5) has souvenirs.

Bengkulu
Goldsmiths in **Kampung Cina**, near Fort Marlborough, work with locally mined gold, while the local speciality textile is called batik besurek, which – unusually for Indonesian textiles – has the pattern hand-painted on after weaving.

Bandar Lampung
Traditional tapis sarongs are now museum pieces. Shops sell less ornate but good-quality fabrics. Try **Lampung Art,** Jl Kartini 12, or **Korpinka Kemala,** Jl Diponegoro Gg. Setiabudi II.

MEDAN	J	F	M	A	M	J	J	A	S	O	N	D
AVERAGE TEMP. °F	80	80	80	80	80	80	80	80	78	78	78	78
AVERAGE TEMP. °C	27	27	27	27	27	27	27	27	26	26	26	26
RAINFALL in	4	4	6	7	10	6	7	7	11	11	9	10
RAINFALL mm	92	108	158	187	248	161	188	171	277	229	229	245
DAYS OF RAINFALL	14	10	15	16	20	14	17	17	23	19	19	19

3
Kalimantan

Land of the **Dayaks** – a collective name for more than 200 tribes – and of vast, ancient rainforests, Kalimantan (the Indonesian part of Borneo) draws the adventurous today as it has for centuries. Many are brought here by the wildlife, the white-water rapids and the untracked depths of the jungle. But for many others the greatest lure is the Dayak people.

A DIVIDED LAND

Providing Indonesia with its longest land-border, the island of Borneo is governed by three separate nations: tiny Brunei Darussalam and the Malaysian states of Sarawak and Sabah in the north, while the lower two-thirds belong to Indonesia. This division was settled by an Anglo-Dutch treaty in 1824, but gave rise to military clashes in 1963 between Sukarno's turbulent Indonesia and the newly independent Malaysia, backed by Britain.

The striking feature of the Dayak cultures is their social organization, with dozens of families living in the same longhouse, which can be over 100m (110yd) long. Each family has its own compartments in the house. People live by agriculture and hunting: many men are still amazingly skilled with the blowpipe, though spears are more common.

Travel anywhere in Kalimantan in the old days was by water, and even nowadays the rivers – massive and slow-flowing as they near the sea, turbulent and fast in the upper reaches – are still important arteries of communication. More often, though, small aeroplanes link remote settlements, landing on rough grassy strips cleared from the forest.

◀ *Opposite: Banjarmasin's floating Kuin Market, on the Barito River.*

DON'T MISS

*** Mahakam River: enjoy an enchanting journey by river bus or houseboat.
** Banjarmasin: buy precious stones – diamonds, emeralds and sapphires – at bargain prices.
* Loksado and the Meratus Mountains: easy treks lead into the hills of South Kalimantan to visit traditional villages.

TREASURES FOR SALE

Beautifully woven rattan baskets, *mandau* (Dayak machetes), and painted war shields make great souvenirs, either from the villages or from Samarinda. Backpack-style baby-carriers are fantastically decorated with beading, bear teeth and claws and wild boar tusks, but genuine ones are rare.

ERAU FESTIVAL

The Erau festival is held in Tenggarong annually, at a different period every year. Dayak tribes from all over East Kalimantan arrive for this cultural festival with dancing, rituals, song and canoe races which celebrates the founding of the town. Unmissable.

Headhunting was practised by some of the tribal groups in the past, with various ritual beliefs associated with the practice. For instance, taking a 'strong' head could guarantee a successful rice harvest and protect a longhouse against disease and other headhunters, and was essential for marriage and funeral ceremonies. Headhunting was eradicated by the joint actions of missionaries and Dutch administrators before World War II, and today young Dayak men leave the longhouse to prove their manhood in the sawmills and oil fields of the coast, sending back televisions and other consumer goods rather than severed heads.

EAST KALIMANTAN

Don't expect to see jungles and tattooed Dayak warriors as soon as you arrive. Decades of logging and forest fires have left scrappy, infertile land cultivated in patches by Javanese settlers, and the economy now depends on the vast reserves of coal, oil and gas, extraction of which leaves inevitable marks on the landscape. However, there are still fascinating cultural trips to be had, especially along the Mahakam River, with some great diving around the Derawan Islands.

Balikpapan and Surrounds

The main arrival point to East Kalimantan is Balikpapan, a wealthy oil city and port. It's a vibrant city, with people having arrived from all over the world to make their fortunes. An interesting visit is to Samboja Lestari, run by the Borneo Orang-utan Survival Foundation, 38km from Balikpapan. There's an ambitious reforestation and research programme under way here as well as a centre for rescued orang-utans. Stay here and volunteer for a few days!

Samarinda

While Balikpapan is founded on oil wealth, Samarinda is East Kalimantan's timber town. The city is cut neatly in half by the mighty **Mahakam River**. Ocean-going freighters travel more than 50km (30 miles) inland to dock within metres of the city's great white-domed mosque, and huge rafts of forest timbers float on the mud-brown waters awaiting their turn at the city's sawmills. You'll also see barges laden with coal heading for the industrial plants of Asia.

Young girls weave intricate sarongs, famous across Indonesia, and 'art shops' sell old and new Dayak carvings and antique china. The city is humid and rather grubby but has a distinctive style of its own, particularly for those wishing to emulate a character in a Joseph Conrad novel.

From Samarinda you can, via the Mahakam, go on epic sorties deep into the interior – or simply take a two-hour boat ride upriver to **Tenggarong**, capital of the old **Kutai Regency**. The **Sultan's Palace** there has been converted into a superb museum with stunning Dayak carvings and ceramics.

The Mahakam River ★★★

There are trips for all budgets. The most comfortable way is to charter a houseboat, while the young and hardy take to the river in a passenger boat – with seating downstairs and mattresses upstairs, standards have improved in recent years.

From Tenggarong the river winds inland through swampy lowlands to the small town of **Muara Muntai**, the last major settlement before you enter the complex of shallow lakes that offer your best chance to see the rare freshwater dolphin of the Mahakam. By the time you get here, the forest is thicker.

▼ *Below: The silhouette of this tract of rainforest near Samarinda is ragged, betraying that the area has been logged.*

▲ Above: Travelling by boat through the Tanjung Puting National Park allows close-up views of the rainforest.

Most visitors detour by motorized canoe across shallow **Lake Jempang** to the Benuaq village of **Tanjung Isuy**, where traditional dance performances are regularly staged. The old, carved longhouse has been turned into a craft centre and guesthouse. Double back to Muara Muntai and then continue upriver to **Melak**, from where jeeps take visitors to the orchid reserve of **Kersik Luwai**. The orchids bloom towards the end of the rainy season, in March or April.

Most tour groups do no more than pay a fleeting visit to this area before heading back to Samarinda or Balikpapan, yet the villages around Melak – and especially around **Barong Tongkok** – are fascinating. Another excursion is to fly up the coast to Tarakan near the Malaysian border, then double back to explore the villages of the Berau Regency and the Krayan Delta. The islands off the coast, centering on Derawan, are a marine reserve; the beaches are used by nesting sea turtles, and coral reefs offer some of the best diving in Indonesia. The Derawan Dive Resort has good facilities.

SOUTH KALIMANTAN
South Kalimantan boasts an interesting city – **Banjarmasin** – as well as diamond mining on inland rivers and some fascinating inland treks amongst Dayak hill tribes.

Banjarmasin *
Lying on the delta of the massive **Barito River**, Banjarmasin is a staunchly Islamic trading city which seems completely at ease with its watery surroundings. Many of the older houses are actually rafts, rising and falling with the tide, while the entire city is crisscrossed with canals and creeks. Enjoy the fabulous sunsets which can dye the peat-heavy waters of the Barito, with its floating mats of water-hyacinth, the colour of blood.

The city acts as a clearing house for the diamond-mining operations of the interior. If you know your stones – and if you are careful – you can buy cut and uncut diamonds, emeralds and sapphires at prices so low you could fund your entire trip from the profits.

Kuin Market, not far from **Trisakti Harbour**, is the largest of Banjar's colourful floating markets, but you have to get there early in the morning: it is virtually over by 08:30. Gorge yourself on sweet, sticky cakes from the floating cafés.

Martapura and Cempaka **

An easy day trip from Banjarmasin, these two towns are the centre of gem mining in South Kalimantan. In **Martapura**, make a point of visiting the town market and nearby diamond-polishing factory – but only buy if you really know what you're looking for!

The Meratus Mountains *

This range forms the spine of South Kalimantan, and they are still dotted with the traditional villages of the Bukit group of Dayaks. Treks lasting anything from a day upwards start from Loksado (four hours from Banjarmasin), from where you can also make an exciting trip along the Amandit River on bamboo rafts – expect to get wet!

CENTRAL KALIMANTAN

Central Kalimantan is emerging as one of the principal nature tourism destinations in Indonesia, with guaranteed orang-utan sightings at Camp Leakey and well-organized river cruises through the rainforest. Most start from Palangkaraya, the provincial capital.

Palangkaraya

This sprawling settlement, on the banks of the Kahayan river, hosts an annual cultural festival in May, the Isen Mulang, celebrating Dayak arts such as canoe-racing and blowpipes.

Rivers and Wildlife

The major draw here is **Camp Leakey**, an orang-utan centre in Tanjung Puting National Park, two hours upstream from Kumai. The orang-utans are well habituated to human beings – most are former captives. A huge area of lowland peat forest and swamp, the park is rich in a variety of other animals too, including crocodiles, otters, sun-bears, gibbons and the entertaining proboscis monkeys. The magnificent bird life is best seen from a *klotok*, or river-boat. There are tours which allow you to travel, eat and sleep on the boat, waking

---

THE INTERIOR

For a foray into the true heartland of Kalimantan, fly in via the jungle airstrip near the Kenyah Dayak village of **Long Ampung**. This is the access point for the magnificent mountains and virgin rainforests of the **Apo Kayan** region. Unless you speak Indonesian, bring a guide with you from Samarinda.

From Samarinda, a road leads north to **Kutai National Park**, which has populations of orang-utans, proboscis monkeys, slow loris, sun-bears and other wildlife despite fires and illegal logging in recent decades. Guided treks and basic accommodation can be arranged from the park headquarters at Sangkimah (three hours by road from Bontang).

◄ *Opposite bottom: A longhouse converted for visitors at Tanjung Isuy using traditional styles and materials.*

KALIMANTAN

▲ Above: Feeding time for the orang-utans at the Tanjung Puting National Park's Camp Leakey.

WEST KALIMANTAN TOURS

Tour providers here are linking with the WWF's 'Heart of Borneo' campaign, offering unforgettable trips up winding rivers into pristine rainforest. Allow at least a week.

KAHARINGAN

Many Dayak were converted to Christianity or Islam, but adherence to the traditional religion – kaharingan – is strong. The government classifies the religion as Hinduism. Many ritual practices are shamanistic, with priests entering a trance and acting as an intermediary to restore harmony between the world of mortals and the spirit world.

to the sounds of the rainforest. There are several other tours from Palangkaraya which cruise the rivers and allow you to spot wildlife and visit traditional villages. In the Sebangau National Park, WWF is working with villagers to provide ecotourism trips – fairly basic at the moment, but a great non-touristy experience.

WEST KALIMANTAN

For years West Kalimantan has had few facilities for tourists, but things are changing. It is now a useful entry or exit point for Indonesia with good land connections to Kuching, Sarawak. Its tourism industry is based on the national parks of **Gunung Palung** and **Betung Kerihun** (formerly Bentuang Karimun). Perhaps more than almost anywhere else in Indonesia, visitors will need fortitude, an adventurous spirit and a reasonable command of Bahasa Indonesia to overcome the challenges of travelling here, since the tourist infrastructure is practically non-existent.

Pontianak

Famous for its sunsets, the provincial capital, Pontianak, is an unpretentious city, bustling with floating markets and coffee shops. The main sights are the **Istana Kadriyah**, the old royal palace, built of ironwood in 1771 and now a museum, and the **Abdurrakhman Mosque**, with its Javanese-style roof. A monument marks the city's location on the Equator. A stroll along the waterfront offers pleasant scenes, but expect to be mobbed by children wanting their photographs taken. **Pinisi Harbour** has lots of Buginese and Javanese schooners, together with huge houseboats which act as floating shops trading up and down the **Kapuas River**.

Pontianak National Museum, built in traditional style, has a good selection of West Kalimantan Dayak costumes and crafts, ceramics and musical instruments. A complete longhouse (known locally as a *betang*) stands in the grounds.

The adventurous can fly to Putussibau, near the Malaysian border, to explore Kapuas Hulu and the Betung Kerihun National Park, where there are still plenty of longhouses. Several conservation organizations are helping local people provide tourism facilities, such as bicycle tours.

GETTING THERE

Fly direct from Surabaya, Jakarta or Sulawesi to Pontianak, Balikpapan or Banjarmasin. Also flights from Singapore and Kuching (Sarawak) to Pontianak and from Singapore to Balikpapan.

GETTING AROUND

A sparse network of roads connects the major coastal cities, but distances are huge and long journeys are best made by air. Inland, transport is either by small aircraft, or increasingly by bus or chartered vehicle as the road network expands. Away from the roads, revert to the rivers – or walk.

WHERE TO STAY

Balikpapan
Hotel Gran Senyiur, Jl ARS Muhammed 7, tel: 0542 820 211, fax: 0542 820 222, www.senyiurhotels.com
Hotel Blue Sky, Jl Letjen Suprapto, tel: 0542 735 844, fax: 0542 424 094, www.blueskybalikpapan.com
Samboja Ecolodge (40km from city), tel: 0542 711 1484, www.sambojalodge.com
For trips along the Mahakam, contact www.adventureindonesia.com and for diving at the Derawan islands see www.divederawan.com

Samarinda
Swiss Belhotel Borneo Samarinda, Jl Mulawarman 6, tel: 0541 200 888, www.swiss-belhotel.com
Aston Samarinda, Jl Pangeran

Hidayatullah, tel: 0541 732 600, www.aston-international.com

Banjarmasin
Mercure Banjarmasin, www.mercurebanjarmasin.com
Swiss-Belhotel Borneo, Jl Pangeran Antasari 86A, tel: 0511 327 1111, www.swiss-belhotel.com

Pontianak
Gardenia Resort and Spa, Jl Ahmad Yani 1, tel: 0561 672 6446, www.gardeniaresortandspa.com
Mercure Pontianak, Jl Ahmand Yani, tel. 0561 577 888, www.mercurepontianak.com
See www.gallery-kapuashulu.org for information on visiting the interior.

Palangkaraya
Excellent cruises on live-aboard river boats can be arranged with WOW Borneo, www.wowborneo.com
For Tanjung Puting National Park, stay at **Rimba Lodge**, tel. 0532 671 0589, www.ecolodgesindonesia.com

SHOPPING

Balikpapan
Look for Dayak handicrafts, woven rattan basketry,

mandau machetes, Penan blowpipes, carvings and some genuinely old ceramics.

Samarinda
Again good for Dayak crafts, although some beadwork items are made by entrepreneurial individuals in the town rather than upriver in the longhouses as tourists fondly imagine. Serious collectors can pick up excellent 'primitive' carvings. If you know ceramics, you may still find 17th- and 18th-century porcelain and Ming, Sung and Khmer funerary ware (including some items stolen from graves).

Banjarmasin
Gems, gems and more gems – with Dayak handicrafts and local tie-dyed textiles called *sasirangan* thrown in for good measure. There are craft and souvenir centres on Jl Sudimampir, along with gem dealers; **Ida**, in particular, is worth a visit – there are some fantastic Ming pieces along with Delft china and old Banjar brassware.

Pontianak
Look for ceramics, Dayak work and hand-woven silks.

PONTIANAK	J	F	M	A	M	J	J	A	S	O	N	D
AVERAGE TEMP. °F	78	78	80	80	82	82	82	82	80	80	80	80
AVERAGE TEMP. °C	26	26	27	27	28	28	28	28	27	27	27	27
RAINFALL in	27	20	13	11	10	8	8	8	10	13	14	18
RAINFALL mm	683	522	330	286	253	199	199	211	271	326	343	465
DAYS OF RAINFALL	18	17	16	22	23	16	20	17	28	30	24	27

4
Java

Java is an island of great natural beauty, despite the challenges posed by the high population. The fertility of the soil, diversity of manufacturing, and industriousness of the people ensure a rising standard of living. With its volcanoes, rice-fields and traditional villages, much of the landscape is still rural – although you need to leave the main roads and towns to enjoy the scenery. In **West Java**, the ancient kingdom of **Sunda**, there is superlative wild scenery, some of it protected by national parks. **East Java** has peaceful hill towns where time seems, if not to stand still, then at least to slow down. And **Central Java** is a fantastic landscape of dramatic volcanoes and river valleys, with clay-roofed hamlets surrounded by groves of fruit trees.

JAKARTA

Capital of one of the world's fastest-growing economies, Jakarta has around twenty million inhabitants – and is expanding almost by the minute. Traffic and air pollution can be ghastly, and the heat and humidity sap your strength. The key to enjoying the city is not to fight its pace and size, its heat, humidity and crowds, but to accept them. It's worth it, for the city has plenty to offer.

Laid out on a north–south axis, Jakarta boasts some of the finest museums in Asia, the remarkable **Taman Mini cultural park**, a fascinating old town (**Kota**) and huge contrasts between the brash new buildings of the main streets and the older residential areas behind them.

CLIMATE

Java can be visited at any time of year, although it is slightly cooler and less humid during the months of June to August. The heaviest rains are normally from December to March). East Java has a drier climate than West Java. Temperatures quickly drop with altitude.

◀ *Opposite: An eruption of Mt Semeru in East Java, with the crater of Mt Bromo in the foreground.*

*** Bogor Botanical Gardens: luxuriant tropical vegetation.
*** Krakatau: possibly the world's most famous volcano – it forms a World Heritage Site with neighbouring Ujung Kulon National Park.
*** Ujung Kulon National Park: primary rainforest where leopards and the last Javan rhinos thrive.
*** Taman Sari: Yogyakarta's exquisite Water Palace.
*** Prambanan: a vast complex of spectacular Hindu temples.
*** Borobudur: The largest Buddhist temple in the world and, like Prambanan, a World Heritage Site.
*** Mt Bromo: a panorama of volcanoes and lava flows.
** Taman Mini: A good introduction to Indonesian cultures with architecture and artefacts from all over.
* Surabaya Old City: Start with the Post Office, an impressive Art Deco building surrounded by other colonial architecture.

Kota (Old Batavia) ***

In the north of the city, Kota (which literally means 'town') is the oldest and most atmospheric part of Jakarta. Here are some of the best museums in Indonesia alongside wonderful old buildings. Aim to spend a full day here, arriving very early to enjoy the cooler part of the day. Start exploring at **Sunda Kelapa**, where hundreds of wooden Buginese ships moor. From the harbour, walk through the lively **Pasar Ikan** ('Fish Market') area to **Museum Bahari**, an interesting and atmospheric maritime museum in two 17th-century Dutch warehouses. Nearby is **Gereja Sion**, Jakarta's oldest church (1695).

Continue to **Taman Fatahillah**, once the main city square of Batavia. The cannon, which used to stand in the square (**Si Jagur**), had to be moved to the courtyard of the Fatahillah Museum to avoid the embraces of local women who believe touching it cures infertility. In a classical colonnaded building is the **Fine Arts and Ceramics Museum** (Balai Seni Rupa), with some paintings, antique porcelain, ancient terracotta statues, and carvings. Cross the square to the beautifully restored 18th-century Dutch **Stadhuis**, now housing the **Jakarta History Museum (Fatahillah Museum)**. In addition to the Si Jagur cannon, there are good displays of the history of Jakarta. Underground are the grim water dungeons where condemned men lay in cells flooded daily by the Ciliwung River. Also on the square is the fascinating **Wayang Museum**, with puppets and costumes from all over Indonesia.

The best time to visit Kota is on a weekend, when there's less traffic. You'll find plenty of local people strolling around and appreciating the open space too. Between visits, take some refreshment at the magnificent Art Deco Café Batavia – not cheap, but well worth the outlay for the ambience!

OUT OF THE CENTRE
Taman Mini **
Taman Mini cultural theme park, 30 minutes by car from central Jakarta offers An overview of Indonesia's myriad cultures. The park, complete with cable car and a huge lake, has exhibitions of arts, architecture and crafts from all of Indonesia's provinces. Inside a giant Komodo dragon is a wildlife museum; the **Indonesia Museum** is equally fascinating. A short walk takes you to a huge bird park with several aviaries.

Ragunan Zoo *
Well worth a visit for anybody interested in Indonesian wildlife. The animals – including gibbons, Sumatran tigers, Komodo dragons and Sumatran rhinoceroses – are kept in large enclosures in a pleasant parkland environment. (The zoo becomes crowded at weekends.)

Textile Museum *
This small museum at Jl Aipda K.S. Tubun No. 2–4 in Tanah Abang has over 600 exhibits from all over the archipelago, including batik and sumptuous *ikat* weaving from Sumba and Flores. Worth a visit if you plan to buy quality textiles later on.

NEARBY
Pulau Seribu (Thousand Islands) *
The coral atolls of the Thousand Island group are almost as perfect on the ground as they look from the air as your plane comes in to land at Jakarta airport. The beaches are white, the water is generally crystal clear and the peace is delicious. The more distant islands – **Putri**, **Pantara**, **Pelangi** and **Kotok** – have cottage-style hotels and diving facilities, with good coral reefs nearby. Transport to and accommodation on all the islands can be booked through most travel agents in Jakarta – advance booking is essential.

▲ *Above: A Dutch colonial building in the Kota district of Jakarta.*

MEDAN MERDEKA, JAKARTA

Get your bearings by locating Medan Merdeka. One of the largest city squares in the world, this is lined with government offices, the **Presidential Palace** and the vast **Istiqlal Mosque**. At the centre is the **National Monument (Monas)**, a 135m (450ft) gold-topped obelisk. A lift inside the tower takes you to the top for a panoramic view of Jakarta.

On the west of the square is Indonesia's **National Museum**. Anybody interested in anthropology, crafts, archaeology or Chinese ceramics could spend days in here. A few minutes away, down Jl Cikini Raya, is **Taman Ismail Marzuki (TIM)**, or the Jakarta Art Centre: this is the city's main showcase for the performing arts, with art galleries, auditoria and a sensational range of performances.

WESTERN JAVA

The ancient kingdom of Sunda, now the heartland of the provinces of West Java and Banten, boasts wonderful mountain scenery, world-famous botanical gardens and national parks such as **Ujung Kulon**, **Gunung Halimun-Salak** and **Gunung Gede-Pangrango**, which protect some fine stands of tropical rainforest. But the long-gone rulers of Sunda built in wood and time has swallowed up the palaces and temples, leaving only the story-telling of the *wayang golek* (wooden-puppet show), enduring folk beliefs, and the secrets of the reclusive Badui people as testimony to a time before Islam.

West Coast

The coastline from Anyer to Labuhan is less than three hours from Jakarta. **Carita Beach** is the oldest seaside resort on the west coast. The many hotels and condominiums here overlook a crescent-shaped bay with silver sand and safe swimming. From here, the ruins of the medieval trading city of Banten can be explored in a day-trip: it has a 16th-century mosque and fascinating remains of palaces and forts.

Krakatau (Krakatoa) ★★★

The original island of Krakatau was vaporized in 1883 in a series of catastrophic explosions heard as far away as Alice Springs in Australia. But this was not its end. In 1928 the island was reborn, emerging from the seas as **Anak Krakatau** ('Child of Krakatau'). It continues to grow, and is now more than 200m (700ft) high. It still has spectacular eruptions. It is usually possible to climb to the crater in a long, hot and dusty slog – but be aware that tourists have been killed in unexpected eruptions. The volcano is surrounded by three smaller islands, surviving fragments of the 1883 cataclysm. There is good snorkelling around some of them, especially Rakata.

Ujung Kulon National Park ★★

The Ujung Kulon peninsula was abandoned after the 1883 tsunami resulting from the eruption of Krakatau. It is the only place in the world where a viable population of Javan rhinos exists – there are around 60 of them. Other animals include leopards, Javan gibbons, wild cattle (banteng), muntjac and sambar deer and green peafowl. Turtles nest in some of the sandy bays. Peucang Island has the best accommodation and wildlife-watching.

Bogor

Sprawling over a plateau and now almost merged with Jakarta, Bogor was a tiny hill village until selected by the Dutch in 1745 as the seat of the first Governor-General of Java. His magnificent palace, the glowing white **Istana Bogor**, now houses Sukarno's art collection. Arrangements to visit have to be made in advance. Known to the Dutch as Buitenzorg ('away from cares'), the city has grown up around the magnificent botanical gardens or **Kebun Raya**. Most tours also take in the **Batu Tulis**, an ancient stone with Sanskrit inscriptions. Beware of the frequent thunderstorms complete with torrential rain – not for nothing is Bogor known as 'City of Rain'!

Natural History Museum *

Natural history aficionados will want to see the collections of birds and animals here. Particularly impressive is the entire skeleton of a Blue whale and a display of venomous snakes. More depressing are the stuffed remains of a Javan tiger (extinct), and the birds, many now very rare in the wild.

From Bogor

Head south to the **Puncak** (*puncak* means 'peak') district to enjoy glorious mountain landscapes and cool air. The scenery is lush and rich, dominated by volcanoes like **Mt Gede** and **Mt Pangrango**, their slopes planted with tea gardens and dotted with bubbling hot springs and good hotels. The **Cibodas Botanical Gardens** are the high-altitude section of Bogor's Kebun Raya and are adjacent to the **Gunung Gede–Pangrango National Park**. Trails here lead amongst well-tended flowers-beds, or up mountain slopes in the national park. Even a day trip here gives a good idea of the rainforest, and for the visitor with more time to spare there are wonderful views and rare plants including giant Javan edelweiss 8m (26ft) high.

▼ Below: Anak Krakatau, the new island rebuilding itself on the site of the volcano that erupted so spectacularly – and so tragically – in 1883.

▲ *Above: A traditional Javanese* gamelan *player.*

HILL FRUIT

The hills around Bandung are high enough to grow European fruits and vegetables, including strawberries (delicious) and apples.

TAXI OR TOUR?

Chartering a taxi for three or four people is often cheaper than booking a tour, and allows you to be more flexible. English-speaking drivers are often quite knowledgeable.

South Coast

From Puncak, take a narrow winding road through the hills to the fishing village of **Pelabuhanratu**, where there are lovely beaches between rocky headlands, holy caves with bats streaming forth like smoke at sunset, and excellent fish restaurants. Be careful swimming here: this is the domain of Nyai Loro Kidul, Queen of the South Seas.

For an adventure, travel south of Sukabumi to the fabulous golden sands of Ujung Genteng. A couple of new hotels make a civilized stay possible. Sea turtles are nurtured in a hatchery: watch the tiny hatchlings scurry across the sand to start their challenging lives in the southern seas.

Bandung

Java's third-largest city, Bandung is home to the **Institute of Technology**, one of Indonesia's best universities, and dozens of other research and teaching institutes. Bandung hosts diverse cultural events – from jazz and rock concerts to classical *wayang golek* puppet performances and traditional Sundanese dance and music. It is a cosmopolitan city with many colonial buildings and good restaurants, but like all big Indonesian cities staggers under the weight of traffic.

West Java is the home of *wayang golek*, or wooden puppets. Performances are usually held Friday and Saturday in the **Gedung Kesenian** – those who lack the stamina for an all-night show can drop out after an hour or two. **Rumentang Siang Theatre** (Jl Ahmad Yani) has frequent performances of *pencak silat*, the Sundanese martial art form, and other lively forms of traditional Sundanese performing arts. The **Yayasan Pusat Kebudayaan** (Jl Naripan 7; off busy Jl Braga) stages *gamelan* or *wayang* performances on Saturday evenings. **Hotel Panghegar** and **Hotel Grand Preanger** stage cultural performances at least once a week with a variety of dance, music and *wayang* – one-stop culture with dinner. Or simply have dinner in the wonderful Art Nouveau dining room of the Savoy Homann Hotel, one of the great hotels of Asia.

Visit **Pak Ujo's 'Bamboo Workshop'** to hear the sounds of the *anklung*, or bamboo orchestra. Students at **SSTI**, the College of Performing Arts (Jl Buah Batu 212), often stage dance performances and concerts, and welcome visitors.

Around Bandung

Head into the hills for stunning mountain scenery, active volcanoes, bubbling hot springs and mud pools. **Tangkubahan Prahu**, about an hour north of Bandung, is Indonesia's only drive-in volcano; visit early before the crowds and the clouds arrive, and take a guide if you want to explore the craters – the crust on some is thin. On your way back, make a detour to **Ciater** via a huge tea estate and visit the nearby hot springs at **Maribaya**. From Maribaya there is an easy two-hour walk back to Bandung through beautiful countryside: the path is straightforward and well maintained (a small charge is levied by villagers who look after it). The walk ends at Dago, a suburb of Bandung, and you can finish off with some refreshments at the quaint Dago Tea House.

Papandayan volcano, near Cisurupan, south of Bandung, has spectacular geysers and is less commercial than Tangkubahan Prahu. The surrounding area is beautiful and tranquil. On your way back from Papandayan, visit the **Malabar Tea Estate**, near Pangalengan.

From Bandung

The road east from Bandung to Garut travels past volcanoes, beautiful lakes and relics of Java's Hindu and Buddhist past. Twenty minutes from Garut the small temple complex at **Situ Cangkuang** ('situ' means 'lake') dates back to at least the 9th century AD. Continuing east to Yogyakarta, the road takes you through the junction town of **Tasikmalaya**, famous for its hats, woven rattan baskets and pretty hand-painted umbrellas. At **Banjarnegara (Banjar)**, allow yourself to be tempted by the beach and head south (two hours) to **Pangandaran**.

Pangandaran *

Two beautiful beaches, a nature reserve, friendly fishermen and delicious seafood … it is easy to stay longer in Pangandaran than you planned. The village is at the neck of a narrow peninsula, now a national park. Fishermen mend their nets on the beaches to the east, while tourists drowse in the sun on the beaches to the west. At holiday times the area becomes busy.

CROWDED ROADS

At weekends the roads to and from the western Java resorts are packed with trippers from Jakarta, so allow plenty of time.

TRAVEL BY TRAIN

Although a fast highway links Jakarta and Bandung in less than two hours, the nicest way to travel is by train (3 hours; several trains daily) from Jakarta's Gambir Station. The trains are slow, rattling and often late, but from air-conditioned Executive Class carriages with their spacious seats you can enjoy views of mountains, ravines, waterfalls and tiny villages. Train schedules can be found on www.kereta-api.com

▼ Below: Fishing boats on Java's west coast seem to have changed little with the centuries.

▼ *Below: A wry smile from one of the retainers at the Kraton in Yogyakarta.*

Pangandaran National Park

There is good snorkelling off the peninsula's beaches and turtles can occasionally be spotted in the pretty coves near **Pasir Putih**. In the park are black leaf-monkeys, muntjac deer (also known as barking deer for their distinctive calls), hornbills, and banteng (wild cattle) feeding in open clearings in the late afternoon. You have to get a permit and take a guide – try and find an older one who knows the animals' feeding and movement patterns.

A popular excursion is the Green Canyon tour, covering small, homely factories making palm-sugar and *krupuk* (prawn crackers), a wayang golek workshop, and a boat-ride upriver into steep-sided gorges which become a giant cavern. Swimming through the turquoise water and leaping from rocks into a deep plunge-pool are unforgettable experiences.

From Pangandaran

Instead of doubling back to Banjar to rejoin the road or take a train to Yogyakarta, go to **Kalipucing** and catch the ferry to **Cilacap**. The journey is four hours of magic through waterways and mangrove swamps – great for birdwatchers, who should see herons, sea-eagles, cormorants and kingfishers. Pangandaran hotels organize ferry tickets and operate a private Cilacap–Yogyakarta minibus service (five hours) linked to the ferry's arrival. An alternative is to travel from Cilacap to **Wonosobo** (two hours), the access point for Dieng Plateau.

Dieng Plateau **

Less visited than Java's other great temple sites, Dieng has the oldest temples in Java, dating back many centuries. High places are sacred in the old Javanese belief system, and the name means 'Abode of the Gods'. In the early morning, with the ground mist swirling about you, there is a haunting, otherworldly atmosphere. Of a city with more than 400 temples and massive flights of steps rising from the valley below, today only eight small temples survive, marooned in a strange, wild landscape of bubbling mud pools, crater lakes and hot springs.

CENTRAL JAVA

This is the Java of the imagination, a land of volcanoes towering over fertile plains dotted with thousand-year-old temples and half-forgotten shrines, a land where *gamelan* orchestras play in royal courts whose rulers trace their line back to a sea goddess – and where some of the finest crafts of the archipelago are produced.

Yogyakarta

For centuries Yogyakarta (Yogya – sometimes written Jogja) was a royal kingdom and powerful trading centre, the seat of the powerful Mataram Empire. The patina of power and pride built up over the centuries still lingers. Today Yogya is best known as a city of culture and the arts. Explore the narrow side-streets to see craftsmen producing exquisite batik and silverwork, visit the Batik Research Centre to see how the craft is being fostered, or haunt the **Kraton** (palace) to watch some of Indonesia's finest dancers and musicians.

The attractions are not only within the city's boundaries. **Borobudur** is less than 2 hours away, while the fantastic temples of **Prambanan** are within half an hour. The energetic can climb one of Indonesia's most iconic (but dangerous) volcanoes, **Mt Merapi** (2911m; 9550ft), menacingly visible from the city. In May 2006 Yogya was struck by an earthquake in which around 5000 people died and many buildings collapsed; most have now been rebuilt.

Palaces ★★★

The **Kraton** (palace) is effectively a city in itself, with batik and silver workshops, mosques, shops and schools enclosed within the 3m (10ft) thick walls. Highlights include the throne-room, ancient *gamelan* and two museums. Classical dance performances and *gamelan* concerts are staged here at least once a week (not during Ramadan).

Taman Sari (the Water Palace), is a series of pleasure gardens built in the 18th century for the sultan and his family. The complex once boasted lighted underwater corridors, underground mosques and meditation platforms.

Pakualaman Palace is smaller but still fine and less visited. *Gamelan* concerts are held here occasionally.

KRATON OPENING HOURS

Don't believe young men in the streets near the kraton in Yogya when they tell you it's closed. The main gates are always closed except for ceremonial occasions – the tourist entrance is round the side. The young men will try to get you to go to their batik workshop instead.

YOGYA SPECIALITY

The *lesehan* (night-stalls) along Jl Malioboro after dark offer excellent local food. Not to be missed is *gudeg*, a delicious local speciality of jackfruit cooked with coconut milk and spices.

PICKPOCKETS

As in Jakarta, be careful – Yogya's pickpockets are extremely skilful. Be particularly watchful around the Post Office, main banks, Water Palace and markets.

▼ Below: The magnificent headdress of a dancer in Yogyakarta.

Loro Kidul and the Sultans of Yogya

According to legend, the Sultans of Yogya descend from a mystical union between the mortal Senopati and the Queen of the Southern Seas, Nyai Loro Kidul. The reigning sultan still pays tribute to Loro Kidul each year with offerings to the goddess at Parangritris in June (the Labuhan festival) and ceremonies on the slopes of Mt Merapi, and she is said to appear sometimes during the sacred Bedoyo Ketawang dance, performed in her honour in the Kraton.

Sonobudoyo Museum, on the square to the north of the Kraton (the Alun-alun), has a comprehensive collection of Javanese arts and crafts. Visit here before you buy batik or other crafts so you can gauge quality.

Cultural Performances

There is a bewildering array of locations for the performing arts of Yogya – from palace to university auditorium to street corner, or your hotel lobby. See classical Javanese ballet, marvellous, intricate *gamelan* concerts, wonderful *wayang kulit* plays and even *wayang orang*, in which people play the parts usually taken by puppets.

Seize any chance to see an episode of the **Ramayana Ballet**. The most magnificent location is the outdoor arena at Prambanan with the floodlit Shiva temple as backdrop. Dozens of fantastically costumed actors and musicians enact the epic, staged on most nights of the year – there's an indoor theatre in case of rain. The full event runs over the course of four evenings; shorter versions are staged all over Yogyakarta.

Around Yogya

Kota Gede was the capital of the Mataram Empire in the 16th century but is now a suburb of Yogya and a centre of fine silverwork. Near the market is the **grave of Senopati**, who founded the city. **Imogiri** (20min) is the burial-place of the royal family and of many sultans of Solo. **Parangtritis** (30min) is a popular beach and centre for the cult of Loro Kidul; offerings are made to the goddess each week. The sea is dangerous – she has set up a strong undertow.

Prambanan

The Buddhist and Hindu temple complexes of the Prambanan Plain are among the finest flowerings of ancient Javanese architecture and for dramatic atmosphere and beauty are the equal of Borobudur. Yet soon after completion, in the 8th–10th centuries, they were abandoned and all but forgotten. Today the major temples have been restored although scores remain to be excavated.

Temple Complex ★★★

Candi Lorojonggrang is the largest and most spectacular of the Hindu temples here. The **Shiva Temple**, 45m (150ft) tall, is the showpiece: it has been partly restored since damage in the 2006 earthquake. It is flanked by the smaller but still magnificent Brahma and Vishnu temples. The interior chambers are decorated with tales from the *Ramayana*, but may still be closed because of earthquake damage.

Walk or take an open-sided bus from Candi Lorojonggrang to **Candi Sewu**, Indonesia's second-largest Buddhist temple complex after Borobudur and now restored to part of its former glory. 'Candi Sewu' means '1000 temples'; in fact the complex consists of 249 shrines surrounding the major temple, which dates back to AD782 and is protected by huge guardian statues.

Other Prambanan Sites ★★

Hire a horse-cart (*andong*) or a bicycle for the day to explore the dozens of other temple sites around Prambanan. They include:

Candi Lumbung, a 10-minute walk from Candi Lorojonggrang. This is a small Buddhist temple surrounded by partly restored shrines.

Candi Sari, on the road from Yogya to Prambanan. Famous for its decorated and carved panels.

Candi Kalasan, just off the main Yogya–Solo road before Prambanan. The oldest Buddhist temple of known date (AD778) in Indonesia.

▼ *Below: Visitors approaching the imposing entrance to Yogyakarta's Kraton.*

THE BATTLE OF SURABAYA

One of the most dramatic battles of World War II in Indonesia was fought in November 1945, three months after the Japanese surrendered and pro-Independence Indonesians raised the national flag. The British fought alongside the Dutch to regain control of the former colony and eventually did so, but the republicans fought bravely and gathered international support as a result – including from the British, who accepted that the drive for independence was not just a minority movement.

JAVA

WAISAK

Borobudur remains one of the holy places of world Buddhism. The annual ceremony of Waisak (usually held around the full moon in May) commemorates the Buddha's birth, death and enlightenment. It starts at Candi Mendut and climaxes around 04:00, when thousands of worshippers converge in a candlelit procession at the summit of Borobudur – a fantastic sight.

TRANQUIL DAWN

Both Borobudur and Prambanan get very busy at weekends. To enjoy these exceptional places to the full, stay locally and arrive early to beat the crowds. Dawn and sunset are times of magic and peace.

CAMERA CARE

Remember to be careful of your camera around Mount Bromo – the fine volcanic dust and ash of the Sand Sea can cause problems, especially to zoom lenses.

▶ *Opposite: Startlingly evocative, the figure of the Buddha is silhouetted against the darkening sky at Borobudur.*

Lush gardens surround these temples. Other sites include the **Ratu Boko temple**, on a plateau with great views over Prambanan and towards Merapi, and **Candi Banyunibo**.

Borobudur ★★★

The world's largest Buddhist temple and the greatest ancient monument in the southern hemisphere, Borobudur is one of the wonders of the world, an artificial mountain of some 60,000m³ (2 million cu ft) of stone. It was built between 778 and 850 – and abandoned soon after completion when the Buddhist Sailendra dynasty was overthrown by Hindu kings. Borobudur was all but forgotten, buried – and protected – by ash from successive eruptions of Mt Merapi until its rediscovery in the early 19th century. Over the next century restoration work was done, and in the mid-1960s a huge archaeological rescue project was launched by UNESCO. In a task comparable with the resiting of Egypt's Abu Simbel statues, Borobudur was literally taken to pieces and rebuilt.

The temple was constructed to resemble India's sacred Mount Meru, with a series of square and circular terraces linked by four main stairways. By turning left upon entering and circumnavigating each tier, you follow the pilgrims' path to the summit, a symbolic journey through the three spheres of Tantric Buddhism. The 5km (3-mile) walk takes you past 1500 relief carvings of the Buddha's teachings and 1200 purely decorative panels. The carvings, a textbook of life in 8th- and 9th-century Java, are studied by historians as well as art lovers. On the upper, open terraces are more than 70 stupas, most containing sitting statues of the young Buddha. Many of the heads are missing, taken over the centuries by collectors, while a few were damaged or smashed during fundamentalist Islamic attacks in 1985.

En route for Borobudur, stop at **Mendut**. The temple here has a statue of the seated Buddha flanked by two acolytes.

Solo (Surakarta)

Vying with Yogya as Java's cultural capital, Solo has all the attractions of its rival: *wayang* theatres and *gamelan* orchestras, wonderful crafts and good food, and two *kratons* – one even larger and older than Yogya's.

Kraton Hadiningrat was badly damaged by fire in the mid-1980s but has been restored. In the palace museum look for Hindu figurines, wedding carriages and a huge wooden statue once carried on the royal barge. The meditation tower was used by the Sultan when he communed with Nyai Loro Kidul. **Kraton Mangkunegaran**, a 10-minute stroll from the main palace, belongs to a junior line of the Solo royal family. Dating from 1757, it hosts one of Java's oldest *gamelan* orchestras, **Jyai Kanyut Mesem** ('Drifting with Smiles'). For most visitors, the museum is the real delight, with wonderful costumes, an excellent collection of masks and a few strange items – including a silver chastity belt. **Radya Pustaka Museum**, next to Sriwedari Park, was founded in the 1890s as the Institute of Javanese Culture and has an excellent collection of old *kris* (wavy-bladed daggers), ancient sculptures and books.

From Solo

Sangiran – a World Heritage Site – is where the first relics of *Homo erectus* were unearthed. A good museum has some interesting exhibits. Java's only erotic temple, **Sukuh**, lies high on the slopes of **Mt Lawu**, with lovely views over the plains. There are good walks in the area, especially the path to Tawang-mangu, emerging by the huge **Grojogan Sewu** waterfalls. A short drive from Sukuh is **Candi Ceto**; beautifully restored, it is built in a series of terraces up a mountainside, with breathtaking views. Sukuh and Ceto were amongst the last Hindu temples to be built before Javanese rulers converted to Islam in the 16th century.

EAST JAVA

Most visitors race through East Java en route for the beaches of Bali, pausing briefly at **Mount Bromo**. But it is well worth lingering here to experience some of the most authentic, pre-Islamic parts of Java.

JAVA SEA

P. Madura

SURABAYA●

EAST
JAVA   Trawas
         ●
        Tretes
         ●
Malang ●
        Mt Bromo ▲

Local men will offer horses for the trek across the Sand Sea. The horses are small but strong, so let them take the strain of the pre-dawn hike. Alternatively, take a jeep or minibus across the Sand Sea and a pony ride for the last few hundred yards uphill through the lava flows. In 2007 a bus terminal was built to keep minibuses and jeeps away from the *poten*, the Hindu temple at the foot of Mt Batok.

▼ *Below: Bull-racing on the island of Madura.*

Surabaya

Surabaya, capital of East Java, is Indonesia's second-largest city. The city administration is doing its best to look after the city: there are wide streets with some fine neoclassical, Art Deco, Arts and Crafts and Art Nouveau buildings. **Surabaya Zoo** has a good collection of Indonesian fauna, particularly birds. Look for the beautiful white Bali starlings (*Leucopsar rothschildi*), one of the world's rarest birds, almost extinct in the wild through trapping for the caged-bird trade. **Perak Harbour** has traditional craft, including Buginese *pinisi* and schooners from neighbouring Madura.

Exploring East Java from Surabaya was hindered for several years by the 'Lapindo mudflow', with millions of litres of hot, acrid mud spewing out because of human error in drilling for gas. It started in 2006 and shows no sign of stopping. New highways have been built to replace the ones destroyed by the mudflow. Malang airport is becoming popular as a hub to travel south and east of Surabaya.

Madura

The island of Madura has fine beaches and ancient mosques, but its real attraction is the bull-racing (*kerapan sapi*). Events are held at least twice a month between April and October with the championships staged in October in **Pamekasan**. Up to 24 pairs of specially bred racing bulls take part in each event, covering 100m (110yd) in just nine seconds.

Malang

Malang is pleasantly cooler than Surabaya, with magnificent scenery nearby. The town has some lovely colonial buildings and good shopping, and is well situated for exploring East Java's ancient Hindu and Buddhist temple sites.

Malang also offers an alternative entry point to the Bromo Tengger Semeru National Park. It is a two-hour drive to

Ngadas, a tiny traditional hill village, and then a half-day walk to Mt Bromo or to Ranu Pani. Ranu Pani is the base for treks up Mt Semeru, Java's highest peak (3676m, 12,060ft). There is excellent trekking all around the hills and valleys here – but stick to the paths or take a guide. It is easy to lose your way.

Kaliandra

Between Surabaya and Malang, Kaliandra (near Prigen) is a good base for exploring the mountains and cultural sites. There are some fine ancient shrines nearby, including beautiful **Candi Jawi, Candi Singosari** and tall, ornately carved **Candi Kidal**. Near Kaliandra is Cisarua Safari Park, worth a visit to see animals from Indonesia and elsewhere (including elephants and tigers) roaming in relative freedom. Take the mountain road via Kediri towards Blitar for fantastic scenery and stop in Blitar to see a typical, unpretentious Javanese town, visit East Java's biggest temple complex at Penataran and the grand grave site of Soekarno, Indonesia's first president.

Mt Bromo ***

Rightly one of Indonesia's great draws, Mt Bromo is best at dawn in the dry season. The volcano lies marooned with its extinct neighbour **Batok** in a sea of ash and lava, the Sand Sea, within the vast caldera of the ancient Tengger volcano. It is an eerie place, especially at night as you cross the Sand Sea to the 250 steep steps leading to the crater rim. As the sun rises over the lava fields, illuminating massive **Mt Semeru** in the distance, silence falls and the power and beauty of nature strike home. To avoid the crowds but still see spectacular views, visit the crater just after sunrise when everyone else has left, or watch the sunrise from the rim of the caldera near Cemoro Lawang village.

Bromo is surrounded by the villages of the Tengger people, who farm potatoes, cabbages and leeks and have retained the Hindu faith which dominated Java until the 16th century.

KASADA FESTIVAL

A number of ceremonies are held at Bromo, many involving sacrifices to pacify the volcano. Most famous is the Kasada, when thousands of people climb the volcano to commemorate their ancestors. Fruit, flowers, chicken and even live water-buffalo are thrown into the crater … or at least into the arms of waiting supplicants – a mutually beneficial arrangement. The date changes each year.

THE FAR EAST

There are several good wildlife reserves in East Java. Most accessible is **Baluran National Park** near Ketapang, ferry port for Bali. The varied vegetation and open savanna offer good wildlife viewing, although acacia trees are encroaching on the grasslands. The volcanic crater of **Ijen** is as spectacular as Bromo and less busy. Alas Purwo has good wildlife and surfing. Less easily reached is **Meru Betiri National Park**, on the south coast, established in a vain attempt to save the last Javan tigers. The main attractions now are the turtle-nesting beach at **Sukamade** and the dense, bird-filled rainforest.

GETTING AROUND

Allow plenty of time to get around: Jakarta's traffic is appalling, although a network of expressways has meant some improvements. Taxis are inexpensive and metered – Golden Bird and Silver Bird are the best (they wait at hotels and the airport or can be ordered by phone, tel: 021 798 1234). Because Jakarta's traffic can be at a near stand-still from early morning to late evening, it can be swifter to catch one of the air-conditioned buses that speed along busways past the stationary cars. *From Jakarta's Soekarno-Hatta Airport:* Registered taxis queue outside the arrivals hall. Unless you know how much the fare should be, shun the pirate cab drivers offering a 'cheaper' deal. Major hotels operate courtesy bus services. Count on an hour into town, but at least 90min to reach the airport from Central Jakarta during the rush hour. If offered a choice by the driver, always choose the expressway (pay for tolls separately from the fare).

Getting Away

By air: Domestic and international flights depart from Soekarno-Hatta.
By train: From Gambir Station to Bogor (90min), Bandung (3hr) and Yogyakarta (10–12hr). The night expresses to Surabaya (via Yogyakarta) depart from Kota Station. Don't waste time queuing for tickets – book through a travel agent.

WHERE TO STAY

Most tourist and international hotels are concentrated in the Central Business District, in the south of the city. If you are only in transit, stay at the Aspac Quality Hotel, tel: 021 559 0008, at Terminal Two, or at the airport Sheraton Bandara Hotel, tel: 021 559 7777.

LUXURY

Borobudur InterContinental, Jl Lapangan Banteng Selatan, tel: 021 380 5555, fax: 021 380 9595, www.hotel borobudur.com Located north of the Central Business District, with everything from an Olympic-size pool to a jogging track.

Le Meridien, Jl Sudirman 18–20, tel: 021 251 3131, fax: 021 571 1633. In the Central Business District.

Hotel Mulia, Jl Asia Afrika Senayan, tel: 021 574 7777, fax: 021 574 7888. Plushly opulent in reds and golds.

Sultan Hotel, Jl Gatot Subroto, tel: 021 570 3600, fax: 021 573 3089, www. sultanjakarta.com The former Hilton, one of Jakarta's first top-class hotels. Good range of facilities.

Hotel Indonesia Kempinski, Jl Thamrin, tel: 021 2358 3800, fax: 021 230 1007, www.kempinski.com/jakarta The oldest luxury hotel in Jakarta.

MID-RANGE

Atlet Century Park, Jl Pintu Satu Senayan, tel: 021 571 2041, fax: 021 571 2191. Centrally located and overlooking a large park.

Grand Kemang Hotel, Jl Kemang Raya 2H, tel: 021 719 4121, www.grand kemang.com South Jakarta.

Ibis Tamarind, Jl Wahid Hasyim 77, tel: 021 315 7706, fax: 021 315 7707. North Jakarta.

Favehotel, Jl Wahid Hasyim 135, tel: 021 392 1002, www.favehotels.com Favehotels is a new chain of mid-range hotels across Southeast Asia – they get very good reviews.

Formule 1 Hotel Cikini, Jl Cikini Raya 75, tel: 021 3190 8188. Good budget hotel in Accor group – clean and well located.

WHERE TO EAT

Jakarta has no shortage of excellent restaurants. Do try the street stalls – anything cooked in front of you is generally pretty safe. Also visit the basements of the big malls, where food is prepared in hygienic surroundings and you can select from different styles of cuisine. For more formal meals, try:

The Oasis, Jl Raden Saleh Raya 47, tel: 021 315 0646. Famous for its *Rijstafel* and stylish surroundings. Booking essential.

Dapur Baba, Jl Veteran 1, tel: 021 7060 2256.

Dapur Sunda, Jl Cipete Raya 13, tel: 021 769 4834.
Pulau Dua, Taman Ria Senayan, Jl Gatot Subroto, tel: 021 570 8906/7. Popular open-air Indonesian restaurant near the Sultan Hotel and Taman Ria Senayan.
Payon, Jl Kemang Raya 17, tel: 021 719 4826. Oasis of tranquillity in busy Kemang; eat Javanese food in gardens.
Sate Khas Senayan, Jl Pakubuwono VI/6, Kebayoran Baru, tel: 021 725 0324.
Ikan Bakar Kebon Sirih, Jl Kebon Sirih, above the excellent **Shalimar Indian Restaurant**, serves barbecued and baked fish.
Jakarta's international-class hotels serve first-rate food. Try:
Bengawan Solo, at the Sahid Jaya Hotel, Jl Jend Sudirman 86, tel: 021 570 4444.
Nelayan, at the Borobudur InterContinental, seafood.

TRADITIONAL ENTERTAINMENT

Bharata Theatre (Jl Kalilio 156, Pasar Senen) offers excellent *wayang orang* (dance) dramas nightly except Monday and Thursday. The **National Museum** and **Wayang Museum** stage superb *wayang kulit* (shadow puppet), *wayang golek* (wooden puppet) and *gamelan* performances on Sunday mornings. **Hotel Borobudur** is among the international-class hotels to stage tradi-

tional dance and music: book for Saturday night dinner and the show is included. Batak singers from Sumatra are known for their harmonies: groups of them serenade diners at several restaurants in the city.

SHOPPING

With arts and crafts from all over the archipelago and huge shopping malls rivalling the best in Asia, Jakarta is a shopaholic's paradise. There is good handicraft shopping at **Sarinah Department Store**, Jl Thamrin. Prices for handicrafts, batik and designer clothes by top Indonesian fashion houses are fixed and reasonable, and the quality is good.

The **Ratu Plaza** mall, in South Jakarta, specializes in computer and electronic goods. **Pasar Seni**, in Ancol, north Jakarta, offers arts/handicrafts. **Pasar Tanah Abang** specializes in textiles. The **Jakarta Handicraft Centre** (Jl Pekalongan 12, near the Hotel Indonesia) sells crafts from across Indonesia. **Keris Gallery** (located at Jl Cokroaminoto 87) has good batik, handicrafts and women's clothes. Other malls are Pondok Indah Mall (I and II), Plaza Indonesia, Taman Anggrek (one of the largest malls in Southeast Asia), Senayan City, and Plaza Semanggi. Full of international brands selling

goods more cheaply than in Europe, most malls have a mix of shops and entertainment facilities. Security is good. The best time to shop is soon after they open, at 10:00 – by late afternoon they are crowded with school children and office-workers.

Antiques

Jl Surabaya is Jakarta's most famous flea and antique market. Doubt any claims of age and authenticity, and bargain hard.
Jl Kebon Sirih Timur Dalam has many interesting antique shops: haggle, despite proprietors' pained looks!
 Jl Pelatehan in the Blok M area is worth checking out but tends to be expensive.
If it's a real treasure hunt you want, it's a good idea to take a taxi to **Situ Gintung** village on Jl Ciputat Raya (the journey takes about an hour), where the road is lined with scores of antique shops and restorers.

TOURS

Tours of Jakarta or around the country can be arranged through **Iwata Nusantara Tours and Travel**, tel: 021 8370 0245, www.iwata-travel.com For more adventurous tours, try the well-established **Adventure Indonesia**, Wisma 31, Jl Raya Kemang 31, tel: 021 718 2250, fax: 021 718 0438, www.adventure indonesia.com

GETTING AROUND

A bewildering choice of airlines link the major cities. More time-consuming but much more interesting are the trains, which go to all major cities, including Bogor. Cars (with drivers) are easily hired everywhere. In **Yogyakarta** take a *becak* – cycle rickshaw – or horse-drawn *andong* to explore the city (check the going rate with your hotel).

WHERE TO STAY

Carita
Hotel Sunset View, tel: 0253 81075, is good value.
Krakatau Seaside, tel: 0253 801 016. Lovely individual cottages in the style of traditional Indonesian houses, on the beach. There are many other guesthouses here.

Ujung Kulon National Park
Tourist-class air-conditioned bungalows are available on Peucang. Tours can be arranged through Java Rhino Tours, tel: 0852 1644 8250, www.krakatautour.com

Bogor
Hotel Santika, Jl Raya Padjadjaran, tel: 0251 850 0707, www.santika.com/bogor
Abu Pensione Hotel, Jl Mayor Oking, tel: 90251 322 893. Friendly service and adequate rooms; budget hotel.

Pelabuhanratu
Samudra Beach Hotel, Jl Raya, tel: 0268 41200 and 41201, fax: 0268 41014. Well away from the village.

Padi Padi Beach Resort, Jl Citepus Raya Km. 13, tel: 0266 432 124, fax: 0266 432125, www.indo.com/hotels/padipadi

Bandung
Grand Hotel Preanger, Jl Asia Afrika 81, tel: 022 4233 631, www.aerowisata.com Beautifully restored colonial-style hotel.
Savoy Homann Hotel, Jl Asia Afrika 112, tel: 022 432 244, fax: 022 436 187. Bandung's stateliest and oldest hotel.
Hotel Bumi Asih Jaya, Jl Soekarno-Hatta 452a, tel: 022 750 8151, www.hotelbumiasih.com Outside Bandung, try the **Sari Ater Hot Springs Resort** at Ciater, tel: 0264 470 894, with a series of hot springs and waterfalls leading down into the valley.

Pangandaran
Over 40 guesthouses/small hotels. **Hotel Komodo**, Jl Baru Bulak Laut 105, tel: 0265 630 753, is friendly and clean. **The Sandaan Hotel**, Jl Pamugaran Bukit Laut, tel: 0265 639 165 or 639 187, has a swimming pool.
Adam's Homestay, Jl Bulak Laut, tel: 0265 639 164, www.adamshomestay.com Away from the beach but quiet and clean.

Ujung Genteng
Turtle Beach Hotel, Ujung Genteng, Sukabumi, tel: 0856 6055 5177, www.turtlebeach resort.com

Wonosobo
Hotel Kresna Wonosobo, Jl Pasukan Ronggolawe 30, tel: 0286 324 111, www.kresna-hotel.com
Surya Asia Hotel, Jl A Yani 137, tel: 0286 322 992, www.suryaasia.com Unpretentious and clean.

Yogyakarta
Hotels and guesthouses here to suit all tastes and pockets.
LUXURY
Phoenix Hotel, Jl Sudirman 9, tel: 0274 566 617, www.accor-hotels.com
Inna Garuda, Jl Malioboro 60, tel: 0274 566 353, fax: 0274 563 074. Very central.
MID-RANGE
Puri Artha, Jl Cendrawasih 36, tel: 0274 563 288.
BUDGET
Hotel Monica, Jl Sosrowijayan, tel: 0274 580 598 or try one of the guesthouses around and along Jl Prawirotaman – some are very good value. Most can organize tours, bus and plane tickets. Just outside the centre is **Rumah Mertua**, tel: 0274 866 680, www.rumahmertua.com

Solo
Kusuma Sahid Prince, Jl Sugiyopranoto 20, tel: 0271 646 356, fax: 0271 644 788, www.kusumasahid.com Super location, vast pool, nightly *gamelan*.
Rumah Turi, Jl Sri Gading Li 12, Turisari, tel: 027 173 6606, www.rumahturi.com
Sunan Hotel, Jl Ahmad Yani 40, tel: 027 173 1312, www.thesunanhotelsolo.com

Surabaya

Hotel Bumi Surabaya, Jl Basuki Rachmad 106–128, tel: 031 531 1234, www.bumi surabaya.com Good quality in fine location.

Majapahit Hotel, Jl Tunjungan 65, tel: 031 545 4333. Fine old colonial hotel.

Novotel Surabaya, Jl Ngagel 173–175, tel: 031 568 2301.

Narita Hotel, Jl Barata Jaya XVII, tel: 031 501 6969, fax: 031 504 5469, www.narita hotel.com Good value.

An excellent restaurant in Surabaya for Indonesian food is **Dapur Desa**, Jl Basuki Rachmat 72, tel: 031 546 3999.

Malang

Pelangi Hotel, Jl Merdeka Seletan 3, tel: 0341 365 156.

Hotel Tugu Malang, Jl Tugu 3, tel: 0341 363 891, www.tugu hotels.com Great quality. While in Malang, eat at the **Inggil** restaurant, Jl Gadjah Mada 4, tel: 034 133 2110. Scruffy but fascinating, and serving good food.

Mt Bromo

Best are the **Lava View Lodge**, tel: 0335 541 009, and the **Bromo Permai**, tel: 0335 541 021. At Tosari, further away but quieter, stay at the **Bromo Cottages**, Jl Raya Tosari, Pasuruan, tel: 031 515 259.

SHOPPING

Bogor

Hand-carved *wayang golek* puppets on offer, as well as gongs and bamboo flutes.

Yogyakarta

Fantastic *batik*, hand-tooled leather, *wayang kulit* puppets, silver, antiques (some genuine), clothes, paintings. **Yogyakarta Craft Centre** has fixed prices; look here first to check prices before going to the markets. For silver go to **Kota Gede**, for instance the factory at Jl Mondorakan 1, tel: 0274 375 107. **Moyudan** village has fine wood carvings. **Jalan Malioboro** has some good items hidden among the tat: you can trust the Batik Keris shops (found in several places). Explore the fantastic **Pasar Beringhardjo** (behind Jl Malioboro), a mass of stalls. Many young batik artists work around the **Taman Sari** area. You will be approached by touts trying to entice you to the workshop of their brother/cousin/uncle – this can be a nice way to buy things since you can then picture where they were made. But beware the difference between waxed batik and printed batik. A good art shop is the Satria Gallery at Jl Rotowijayan KP II/64, tel: 081 128 6743. They sell an excellent range of *batiks*, masks, *wayang kulit*, and other Javanese artefacts.

Bandung

Wayang puppets and masks, superb ceramics (convincing copies of ancient Chinese porcelain), paintings, sculpture; musical instruments.

Solo

Jl Secoyudan has goldsmiths' shops. You can visit **Sriwedari**

Park for presents (especially handmade toys), antiques – from genuine to obviously fake – and handicrafts in the **Pasar Triwindu** fleamarket. There are handmade *wayang kulit* puppets at **Manyaran**, where a dozen or so craftsmen work. For batik visit **Pasar Klewer**, near Susuhunan Palace.

Surabaya

Surabaya has huge shopping centres such as **Tunjungan Plaza** and **Delta Plaza**. **Jl Basuki Rachmat** is good for curios and antiques. Also worth a visit is the colourful **Kayoon Flower Market**.

TOURS

If you want to visit **Krakatau**, the hotels in Carita can organize tours.

At **Bogor** the tourist office, Jl Veteran 2, just off Jl Juanda, has a great range of excursions and activities; useful maps. In **Bandung** the tourist offices are Bandung Visitor Centre, Jl Asia Afrika, tel: 022 446 644, and West Java Tourist Office, Jl Cipaganti 15. The **Wonosobo** tourist office, Gedung Sasana Bhakti 45, has maps, suggested walks, and lists of nearby attractions. In **Yogyakarta** the tourist office is at Jl Malioboro 16, tel: 0274 566 000. The **Solo** tourist office is at Jl Slamet Riyadi 275. The **Surabaya** tourist office, Jl Pemuda 118, tel: 031 567 5448, has information on events such as Madura bull-races. The **Malang** tourist office is at Jl Tugu 1.

5
Bali

The shimmering green jewel in Indonesia's crown of islands, Bali has epitomized tropical paradise for decades. This is an island of soaring volcanoes, of rice terraces tumbling down the hillsides in sculpted tiers, of fantastic Hindu temples and age-old dances, of glorious beaches and sybaritically luxurious hotels. No longer just the haunt of culture buffs and surfers, Bali offers excellent golf courses, sophisticated dining, spas, yoga classes, night clubs, trendy shopping outlets, and outdoor activities from bird-watching and hiking to paragliding, white-water rafting and diving.

It all began in the 1930s, when Bali began to come to the attention of the rest of the world as a series of European artists – such as Rudolf Bonnet and Walter Spies – settled here and wrote home with tantalizing pictures of an island paradise in which every man was a painter, sculptor or musician and every woman a dancer. Now, the island is truly international, catering to tourists from the richer Asian countries, Russia and other parts of Indonesia as well as Europeans and Australians.

Beneath the globalized veneer, however, religion still permeates all aspects of Balinese society: every home and office has a shrine where daily offerings to the spirits are made, and behind every hotel reception desk, on the dashboard of every minibus, one thing remains a constant – a small offering adorned with fresh flowers and rice. The Balinese worship the same trinity – Brahma, Shiva and Vishnu – as Hindus in India, although with the addition of local beliefs. For the Balinese, gods and good spirits live in the mountains while demons and giants lurk in the sea; they seek to maintain a balance between these two extremes, honouring the good and placat-

CLIMATE

The rainy season runs roughly Nov–Mar, with the heaviest rainfall in Dec–Jan. May–Sep is generally dry, with brilliant blue skies – although expect a few tropical downpours, usually in the late afternoon. But there is another factor to consider when timing your visit: of the island's annual two-million-plus visitors, most descend in Jul, Aug and Dec.

◄ *Opposite: The main street of a Balinese village shows in microcosm that this is an island like no other!*

73

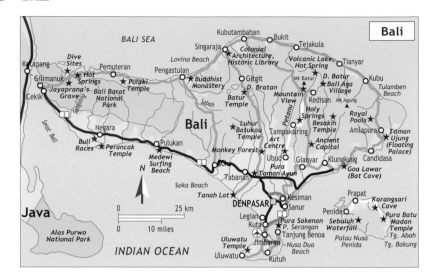

ing the evil. There are temples everywhere and most villages have at least three: a *pura puseh*, dedicated to the founders of the village, a *pura desa*, for the spirits that protect the village, and a *pura dalem*, the temple of the dead.

Ceremonies and festivals are another integral part of Balinese life and culture, with at least five or six festivals annually in every village. Each stage in life – pregnancy, birth, puberty, marriage and death – has its ritual. Among the best known is the tooth-filing ritual, carried out at puberty, when teeth are filed smooth to produce an even dentition – only demons have crooked fangs. Funerals are spectacular affairs in which the body is carried to its crematory pyre in a bamboo or wooden tower. These may be huge, requiring dozens of men to carry them. The bearers run to the cremation-place, twisting and turning every few metres, moving around in circles – a trick intended to confuse the dead person's spirit so it cannot return to haunt the family.

Balinese Dance

Less formal and more dramatic than the stately court dances of Java, Balinese dance is an art form for the people. Virtually every village has its own dance troupe, and young girls

▶ *Opposite: Beauty, youth and grace are just some of the characteristics of Balinese dance.*

dream of becoming a great Legong dancer. Look out for village festivals, which usually culminate in dance performances. The main dance-forms are:

Kecak: Often called the Monkey Dance, this relates the legend of the abduction and rescue of Rama's wife Sita. A massed choir – whose monkey-like chanting gives the dance its name – forms the backdrop.

Barong: A brilliant dance narrative that veers from pantomime to high drama as a huge lion-like holy animal (the Barong) does battle with the evil witch Rangda. Best seen in the villages, where people really enter into the spirit.

Legong: Considered by the Balinese the most complex and graceful of all dances. The dancers are usually two young girls who are trained from the age of 5 and retire at 13.

Sanghyang (trance) dances: These probably date back to pre-Hindu exorcism rites. Most spectacular are the Fire Dance, when men trample unharmed on burning coconut shells, and a Legong-style dance in which two young untrained girls dance in unison – with their eyes shut.

THE SOUTH

Bali's original and most lively resorts are centred south of Denpasar, although there are now resorts all over the island. Most of the major temples and craft villages are an easy half-day's excursion from the main resorts.

Denpasar and Surrounds

The island's capital is a working city: noisy and chaotic, but there are several places very much worth visiting. The beautiful **Bali Museum (Museum Negeri)** at Jl Letkol Wisnu 8 (next to Pura Jagatnatha) is built in a series of open pavilions, with examples of both palace (*puri*) and temple (*pura*) architecture. (Open daily; wear long trousers, a sarong or skirt.) The **Art Museum** (Jl Abian Kapas) has three galleries with exhibitions of paintings and woodcarving. Regular dance performances are staged here. In the evenings the **Night Market** behind the Kumbusari Centre has hundreds of stalls selling delicious food.

Not far from Denpasar, **Tanah Lot**, Bali's most photographed sea temple, is a short drive west of Legian.

Pura Taman Ayun, surrounded by a moat, is the old state temple of the former kingdom of Mengwi and another easy drive from the peninsula. In **Sangeh**, the temple is located just outside the village, around 30 minutes from Denpasar. The forest, complete with nutmeg grove, is said to have been dropped by the Monkey God Hanuman as he flew off to do battle with the evil Rawana. Keep a firm hold of your possessions – the monkeys are light-fingered. They particularly like spectacles and will snatch them from your face.

Kuta, Legian, Seminyak, Tuban and Jimbaran

Once simple fishing villages set on a palm-fringed beach, **Kuta, Legian** and **Seminyak** have merged to form Indonesia's biggest resort, with a huge range of hotels. The commercialism can be offputting – although the shopping is excellent, especially in Seminyak. The southern fringe of Kuta is called **Tuban**. South of Tuban, on the other side of the airport, **Jimbaran** is a beautiful bay with white-gold sands and several up-market hotels and spas.

Sanur

Stretching out along a reef-protected beach on the eastern side of the Badung Peninsula, Sanur has attracted Western visitors since the 1930s, when it was a haunt of the artists who 'discovered' Bali. Developed since the 1960s as the smart alternative to Kuta, it now has dozens of luxury hotels – although more reasonably priced accommodation can be found here in smaller establishments.

The resort has, though, retained some of its Balinese identity. Outrigger canoes are still pulled up on the beach and kite-flying competitions are held in the beach-side fields beyond the hotel strip. There is good beginners' snorkelling on the coral reef, but swimming in the shallow bay becomes difficult at low tide. Be careful paddling: coral grazes don't heal easily, and there are sea urchins. Also, the coral is easily damaged and can take years to recover from trampling.

The former home of the Belgian artist **Jean Le Mayeur**, who lived in Bali from 1932 till his death in 1958, is now a museum where a restoration programme has preserved his works. They depict a Balinese lifestyle now fast disappearing.

▶ *Opposite: The silver sands of Kuta Beach draw holiday-makers from all over the world.*

The museum is right next to the Bali Beach Hotel, built in the early 1960s as the island's first luxury hotel, and the only one taller than a coconut palm.

Nusa Dua

A few miles south of Sanur is Nusa Dua, an enclave of luxury hotels developed to attract the high-spending package tour market. The beaches are good and the hotels are sumptuous, with good shops and restaurants. Tours can be arranged from here to destinations all over Bali and beyond.

Around the Peninsula

Ulu Watu Temple overhangs the towering cliffs at the southern tip of the peninsula. Most people come at sunset, but the temple is spectacular any time. Nearby **Suluban Beach** has fantastic white sand and regularly features in surfing movies.

Nusa Penida Island, drier and less fertile than the Bali mainland, is visited by thousands of Balinese on pilgrimages to avert bad luck: the island is home to evil spirits. There are a couple of interesting temples, and some good beaches and diving. A turtle conservation programme hatches and releases baby sea-turtles and there's also a successful breeding programme for the beautiful but endangered Bali Starling.

Lembongan, just two hours from Sanur by boat, has become popular. There are some lovely pale gold beaches, good coral and fantastic views of **Mount Agung**.

Ubud

European artists like Spies who settled here in the 1930s encouraged young local artists to break away from the formal Balinese temple and court art and experiment with new images and forms. The village has expanded dramatically: there are now roads and unbroken lines of shops and hotels where 30 years ago there were only rice paddies, and Ubud has merged with surrounding hamlets like **Peliatan**, **Campuhan** and the painting village of **Penestanan**. There are some superb restaurants, and opportunities abound for spiritual and physical healing: look for yoga classes, Ayurvedic medicine or a bewildering range of spa treatments, from Javanese deep muscle massage to hot stones.

MAIN RESORTS

- **Sanur:** Bali's first up-market beach resort, and still stylish. The sea is too shallow to swim at low tide.
- **Nusa Dua:** On the east coast of the southern peninsula, a purpose-built enclave of international-class hotels.
- **The Kuta/Legian strip:** On the southern peninsula's west coast, the liveliest resort. Famous sunsets, surf, shopping and nightlife, but noisy and commercial, and with dangerous waters.
- **Tuban:** To the south of Kuta and slightly quieter and more up-market.
- **Jimbaran:** further south again, with some beautiful beach hotels.
- **Candidasa:** Once a backpackers' haven, now a fully fledged alternative to Legian and Tuban.
- **Ubud:** Still the cultural heart of the island, set in the hills amid breathtaking scenery, although now a busy town rather than a quiet village and with some nightlife.
- **Lovina:** On the north coast; a slightly more relaxed alternative to the busy southern resorts.

▼ Below: In Ubud there are so many dance troupes that it is not hard to find a performance of one of the classics – or even an impromptu street display.

Culture still features strongly, however: there are as many art galleries and working studios in Ubud as bars and souvenir shops, and with dozens of local dance troupes, it is easy to find high-class performances of the Balinese classics. In Ubud itself there are performances several nights a week, and tour operators sell transport-inclusive tickets to performances at nearby villages like **Bona** and **Peliatan**. Signboards advertise what is on offer and ticket-sellers tour the streets.

Rice Terraces

There is so much concern about the possible loss of the rice terraces, becoming neglected because the Balinese earn more through tourism, that some people grow rice even though it is no longer economically necessary. In 2012 a group of Balinese intellectuals succeeded in their bid to have the complex system recognized as global cultural heritage with UNESCO. Explore the rice terraces near Ubud by heading off the beaten track on foot, or ask a guide from your hotel to take you.

Around Ubud ★★

Puri Lukisan art museum has comprehensive exhibits of all the schools of Balinese painting in a series of pavilions set in lovely gardens. The **Neka Art Museum**, in Campuhan, specializes in modern Balinese art (some pieces are for sale). The well-managed **Monkey Forest**, with its network of paths and polite monkeys which take bananas gently from your fingers, is a 15-minute stroll from the main square, along Monkey Forest Road. There is a small Temple of the Dead in the forest. Follow the paths and steps downhill to find a quiet stream gorge with shrines to the spirits of the springs. **Peliatan**, 2km (just over 1 mile) south of Ubud, is among the most important dance centres in Bali, with two or more performances a week. **Pengosekan** (a 10-minute walk from Peliatan) has many painters; most are delighted to show their work.

One of the nicest expeditions around Ubud is the walk or cycle ride to **Petulu**, where thousands of white egrets roost at night (the birds start to fly in around 16:00). A shorter but no less beautiful walk is down to **Yeh Agung Gorge** at Kedewatan or Sayan. A slightly longer walk on a well-marked trail (take a guide if you are not sure) takes you east from Ubud to the deep **Sungai Petanu** gorge, where you can clamber down to the Goa Gajah cave shrine or walk up to the temples around **Pejeng**.

North of Ubud is the **Elephant Safari Park**, with botanical garden and **Sumatran** elephants which give elephant rides.

Bedulu to Tampaksiring ★★★
Between Bedulu and Tampaksiring are more than 30 of Bali's oldest temples and shrines. Explore the area as a day-trip from Ubud: start at Tampaksiring, then slowly make your way back. Many of the paths involve steep climbs up and down.

Gunung Kawi has 11th-century temples and tombs carved into a solid rock face. Get here early to savour the atmosphere. **Tirta Empul** has springs said to prolong life and ease sickness; many Balinese come here on pilgrimage and it can get hectic. In Pejeng, visit **Pura Kebo Edan** ('Crazy Buffalo Temple'), with brilliant carvings and statues, one with six penises. **Pura Penataran Sasih**, the old state temple of Pejeng kingdom, houses the 3m (10ft) long Bronze Age drum known as the **Moon of Pejeng**.

Goa Gajah ('Elephant Cave') was named for the huge demon that forms the temple's mouth. The carvings around the entrance are monstrous and surreal. **Yeh Palu**, a 20min walk (signposted) from Goa Gajah, is more peaceful, a frieze 9m (30ft) long carved on a cliff-face. You might have it to yourself: most groups only walk a few metres along the track.

CENTRAL BALI AND THE MOUNTAINS
Mt Batur ★★
You have only to fly over Bali or look at a relief map of the island to realize the central mountains account for much of the territory. The highest – and holiest – point is the currently dormant **Mt Agung** (3142m; 10,308ft). A greater attraction for many is **Mt Batur** (2276m; 7467ft), also a dormant volcano, which towers above Lake Batur and the village of Trunyan.

An easy drive from Ubud or a day-trip from Sanur or Nusa Dua, Mt Batur comprises an ancient caldera out of which a younger volcano has risen. **Lake Batur** lies at the foot of the mountain, taking up most of the old caldera.

▲ *Above: It is not hard to see how Ubud's Lotus Café got its name.*

The drive from Denpasar into the hills around Ubud leads through some of Bali's best craft villages. Shops line the main road, but explore the backstreets to see items actually being made.

Batubulan, 10min north of Denpasar, is best known for its stone carvings and sculptures, some small enough to carry or ship home. The village hosts a daily Barong performance which is well choreographed and presented. **Celuk**, beyond Batubulan on the road to Ubud, is Bali's best-known silverworking centre; backstreet silversmiths will make pieces to order.

Sukawati is a busy market village, an interesting place to explore, though most coach parties drive straight through on their way to Ubud or Mas. The Pasar Seni art market is worth a look, as are the workshops making wind-chimes and temple umbrellas. The old Sukawati Palace is hidden behind the shops.

Batuan, between Sukawati and Mas, is a painting centre. Shops also sell ornately carved wooden panels and screens. **Mas**, Bali's biggest carving centre, is particularly known for its masks; prices are lower in the afternoon, when the morning coach parties have left. **Gianyar** is the island's biggest weaving centre, with dozens of factories producing everything from traditional sarongs to T–shirts to high fashion items.

Stop off at **Penelokan**, on the very lip of the old caldera, for fantastic views over the lake. At night (it can be very cold, both here and in Bratan) the moon seems to float on a level with Mt Batur's crater.

Around Lake Batur

Trunyan is a village of the Bali Aga, the original inhabitants of Bali; the lakeside setting is lovely but get a guide to organize the trip for you. The Bali Aga do not cremate their dead but place the body in open bamboo cages to decompose. The graveyard is along the lake (by boat) at **Kuban**.

Tirta, on the lakeshore opposite Trunyan, has hot springs and is a good base for the three-hour climb to Batur's peak.

Lake Bratan ★★

High in the mountains on one of the few passes through the island, Bratan, like Batur, is a crater lake set in glorious scenery, with tree-covered mountains rising on all sides. It is very peaceful, especially around the nearby smaller lakes (water-skiing is available on the main lake).

Nearby, **Pura Ulu Danau** is dedicated to Dewi Danau, goddess of the waters. The dedication is appropriate: though the main part of the temple is built on a small peninsula, two smaller buildings are set on islands in the lake. The **Eka Karya Botanical Gardens** are an offshoot of the main Botanical Gardens in Bogor (see page 57); watch for the turn-off close to Candikuning (which has a good market). **Bali Handara Kosaido Country Club** has a world-class 18-hole golf course.

Return from Bratan to the south coast on the road via **Pupuan** to see clove and vanilla plantations and some of Bali's most immaculate rice terraces.

Batukaru ★

One of the holiest temples in Bali, set in the western part of the central hills, Batukaru is surrounded by huge, ancient trees and emanates an atmosphere of powerful sanctity.

Mt Agung

Dominating the east coast, Agung is the island's highest and most revered mountain: a haunt of the gods, and site of

Besakih, largest and holiest of all Bali's temples. The volcano is currently dormant, but in the last major eruption in 1963, 2000 people died and tens of thousands lost their homes.

Besakih Temple ★★★

Built high above the coast, with fantastic views towards Lombok and Mt Rinjani, Besakih is actually a complex of 22 temples. Built on a series of ridges, its flights of steps and courtyards lead worshippers upwards to the main spire, located at the highest point, closest to the seat of the gods. It is approached via a long flight of stairs dominated by the temple's tall black pagodas.

THE EAST

Historically home to some of the island's most powerful kingdoms, eastern Bali probably has more important temples and palaces than any other part. Start exploring at **Klungkung**, for 300 years the capital of Bali's most powerful kingdom, **Gelgel**, now a slightly frantic junction town, but distinguished by the ornate Balinese architecture fronting the shop-houses. **Kerta Gosa**, the Hall of Justice, can get busy. The open pavilion has a painted ceiling depicting sinners being tortured by demons on the lower levels while the innocent enjoy the pleasures of heaven above. A few metres away is the **Bale Kambang**, the Raja's floating pavilion. **Goa Lawah** (20min from Klungkung) is one of Bali's nine most sacred temples, a cave fronted by a shrine 'guarded' by thousands of bats. The temple was renovated in 2007 and is now a large complex.

Padang Bai

Chiefly known as the ferry port for Lombok, Padang Bai is developing a tourism industry. There are small bays and beaches on either side of the main ferry port bay, such as the pretty Blue Lagoon bay, which just has room for two small cafés renting out sunbeds and snorkelling equipment. Above it is an up-market development of gorgeous villas.

Candidasa

In the early 1980s Candidasa was a tiny fishing village with a small temple and lotus pond, a lagoon and a couple

▲ *Above: Moody Lake Batur, renowned for its superb views.*

BALI BIRD WALKS

To enjoy the finest scenery in Bali, coupled with an introduction to the birds and butterflies, take one of the Bali Bird Walks (every Tuesday, Friday, Saturday and Sunday) from Campuhan, Ubud. Led either by the classically eccentric Englishman Victor Mason or the knowledgable and lively Su. Young coconuts consumed en route and lunch at the renowned Murni's Warung are included; tel: 081 239 13801 or 0361 975 009, www.balibirdwalk.com

Two main routes go through the mountains, one passing Lake Bratan and the other Lake Batur. A popular round trip is:
- drive up to Kintamani and Penelokan
- stop off at Lake Batur
- continue to Bali's north coast
- double back into the mountains near Singaraja
- return to the south coast via Lake Bratan

It is just possible to do this in a day, but staying overnight at Lovina, Tirtagangga or Bratan is much pleasanter.

of backpackers' hostels. Now, there are scores of guest-houses and some smart hotels. In place of peace and simplicity it has good facilities – from car-hire and money-changing to a good choice of restaurants. The temple is still there, and so is the lagoon, while over the headland you can catch magical tropical sunsets.

Around Candidasa

Tenganan is, like Trunyan, a Bali Aga village and can get very busy. Unlike Trunyan, however, the villagers are quite friendly. Tenganan, still partly fortified, is famous for its rituals and ceremonies and for its unique *grinsing* weaving. As a result of tourist interest and a tenacious adherence to its traditions, Tenganan is a strong and wealthy community.

Amlapura, on the eastern tip of Bali and an easy outing from Candidasa, is the site of an ancient kingdom with not one but three palaces. **Puri Kanginan** is the largest, but much more beautiful are the water palaces built in the 20th century by the last Raja of Karangasem. At the village of **Ujung** are the remains of his first project, a small lake surrounded by pavilions representing the sun and moon. Better still is the **Tirta Gangga** water-palace, a 30-minute drive north of Amlapura. Surrounded by some of the most incredible rice terraces in Bali, it's a wonderful place to stay for a couple of days. Originally created for the royal family, nowadays everyone can enjoy the refreshing waters of the magical pools.

THE NORTH

With mainly black sand beaches and a drier climate, Bali's north coast became popular with tourists much later than the south. The area fell to the Dutch almost 60 years earlier than the south, and, while Balinese Hindu culture survives here, it has been tempered by longer contact with the outside world.

There is an excellent range of accommodation, from up-market hotels to simple guesthouses where a night's stay costs less than a snack lunch in one of the luxury resorts of Nusa Dua.

The centre of Dutch colonial power in Bali until independence, **Singaraja** is the biggest town in the north, with two colleges and a library of ancient manuscripts.

▼ *Below: A long-tailed macaque stares back with frank interest from the Balinese forest.*

Lovina Beach and Surrounds *

The coastal villages west of Singaraja are known collectively as **Lovina Beach**. The calm waters make swimming along the reefs, just offshore from the beach, a delight, and an early-morning trip by outrigger canoes, with

▲ *Above: Mt Batur looms above the lake of the same name, itself formed in an old volcanic caldera.*

the sun rising and the possibility of watching dolphins playing, is unforgettable.

Banjar, Bali's only Buddhist monastery, is up in the hills, just outside the village of **Banjar Tega**. **Sawan**, inland to the east of Singaraja, is a small craft village specializing in gamelan instruments. Off **Tulamben**, at the northern tip of the east coast, is the wreck of a Liberty class ship torpedoed by a Japanese submarine in 1942; now home to reef fish and coral growths, this is one of Bali's most popular dive sites.

THE WEST

Mountainous, heavily forested and wild, huge areas of western Bali are now within the magnificent **Bali Barat National Park**. This is one of the few parts of Bali where you can still feel like an adventurer, where the local people are surprised – and delighted – to see a Western face. Comprising nearly 80,000ha (176,000 acres) of forest, steep-sided mountain and coral reef, the park is a huge commitment to conservation. One of the world's rarest birds, the brilliant white Bali Starling with dark blue markings, has its home in the lowland forests here. Local legend speaks of lost cities and temples and of the Bali tiger (now extinct). The National Park Office is at **Cekik**, at the junction of the road from Lovina with the road to the ferry port of Gilimanuk. Staff can organize short – or long – jungle treks.

PROTECTED REEF

Menjangan Island, reached from Labuhan Lalang, is part of the Bali Barat National Park, and its magnificent coral reefs are protected. The area has Bali's best diving.

RETIREMENT AND SECOND HOMES

Indonesia now offers a year-long retirement visa for people over 55 who wish to spend their declining years (and their foreign exchange) in the country. Second homes can be bought on a lease arrangement. Villas often come complete with plunge pools, sea views, on-site restaurants and spa services. Check the legalities and rate of return carefully.

BALI AT A GLANCE

GETTING THERE

By air: Bali's airport, **Ngurah Rai**, is on the south coast near the main resorts.

By sea: Ferries from Java arrive at **Gilimanuk** on the far west coast, and from Lombok they dock at **Padang Bai**. The 4hr ferry ride from Lombok is a pleasant trip, although the hydrofoil to Benoa from Senggigi is much quicker.

Cruising: Several cruise ships operate around Bali and on to other islands, especially the Lesser Sundas; you can travel on anything from a luxury liner to a wooden sailing ship. For schedules and prices, try www.balicruises.com

GETTING AROUND

Tour operators offer a host of excursions and activities. Even for independent travellers, these are a helpful introduction to Bali. Bali Adventure Tours provides excellent insights into the island through activity holidays. Contact them via www.bali adventuretours.com

Many tourists use the public-transport **minibuses** (*bemos*) which operate all over the island on prescribed routes, while **hire cars** or **jeeps** allow exploration of narrow mountain roads inaccessible to tour coaches. Self-drive is a definite possibility in Bali. You will need an International Driving Licence to hire a car.

WHERE TO STAY

There is accommodation to suit all tastes and purses in Bali,

including some of the best hotels in the world. The website bali blog.com has useful tips.

Sanur and *Nusa Dua*

Sanur Beach Hotel, tel: 0361 288 011, www.sanur-beach-hotel.com

Respati Bali, Jl Danau Tamblingan 33, Sanur, tel: 0361 288 427, www.respati beachhotel.com Mid-range.

Amanusa, Nusa Dua, tel: 0361 772 333, www.amanresorts.com Expensive and up-market.

Grand Mirage Resort, Jl Pratama 74, Tanjung Benoa, tel: 0361 771 888, www.grandmirage.com

Conrad Bali, Jl Pratama 168, Tanjung Benoa, tel: 0361 778 778, www.conradbali.com

Legian and Surroundings

The Amala, Jl Kunti 108, Seminyak, tel: 0361 738 866, www.theamala.com

The Kayana, Jl Raya Petitenget, Kerobokan Kelod, Kuta Utara, tel: 0361 847 6628, www.thekayana.com

Villa de daun, Jl Raya Legian, tel: 0361 756 276, www.villadedaun.com

The Semaya, Jl Laksmana, Seminyak, tel: 0361 731 149, www.thesamayabali.com Luxury beachside villas with spa.

Hotel Tugu Bali, Jl Pantai Batu Bolong, Canggu Beach, tel: 0361 731 701, www.tugu hotels.com Private villas and spa set in lush gardens.

Poppies Bali, Jl Poppies 1, tel: 0361 751 059, www.poppies bali.com

There are hundreds of small hotels and guesthouses along the Kuta/Legian strip. Many are excellent value, but few are on the beach.

Tuban

Bali Dynasty, Jl Kartika Plaza, tel: 0361 752 403, www.bali dynasty.com

Sandi Phala, Jl Wana Segara, tel: 0361 753 780.

Jimbaran

Four Seasons Resort, tel: 0361 701 010, www.fourseasons.com

Jimbaran Puri Bali, tel: 0361 701 605, www.jimbaranpuri bali.com

Udayana Ecolodge, tel: 0361 747 4204, fax: 0361 701 098, www.ecolodges indonesia.com An eco-friendly hotel on the hill above Jimbaran Bay.

Tabanan

Sarinbuana Lodge, tel: 0361 743 5198, www.bali ecolodge.com Cottages on the edge of rainforest.

Ubud and Surroundings

Komaneka Resort, Monkey Forest Road, tel: 0361 976 090, www.komaneka.com

Ubud Village Hotel, Monkey Forest Road, tel: 0361 975 571, www.theubudvillage.com

The Ina Inn, Jl Bisma, tel: 0361 971 093. Good value.

Ubud Hanging Gardens, in Desa Buahan, has luxury villas, tel: 0361 982 700, www.ubudhanginggardens.com

The Waka Namya Resort, tel: 0361 975 719, www.wakanamya.com Particularly welcomes children.

Lake Bratan

Bedugul has small hotels and guesthouses around the lake e.g. the **Strawberry Hill Hotel** (tel: 0368 21265, www.strawberryhillbali.com), and the **Lila Graha**. To experience village life in a degree of comfort, go to **Puri Lumbung**, in Munduk village, tel: 0362 92810, www.purilumbung.com Activities from Balinese massage to trekking can be arranged from here.

Candidasa and East Bali

The Water-Garden (Hotel Taman Air), Jl Candidasa Raya, tel: 0363 41540, www.watergardenhotel.com Centrally located, with pretty gardens. **Alam Asmara Dive Resort**, Jl Candidasa Raya, tel: 0363 41929, www.alamasmara.com **Kubu Bali**, tel: 0363 41532, www.kubu-bali.com Secluded bungalows. **Bloo Lagoon Village**, Padangbai, tel: 0363 41211, www.bloolagoon.com **Bali Homestay**, tel: 081 7067 1788, www.bali-homestay.com Well-run budget accommodation in villages.

Lovina Beach

Lovina Beach Houses, Jl Kartika, tel: 0821 4732 3655, www.lovinabeachhouses.com **Hotel Banyualit**, tel: 0362 41789, www.banyualit.com

Saraswati, Kalibukbuk, tel: 0362 41462, www.saraswati-bali.com Just two bungalows in tranquil gardens.

West Bali

There are several boutique resorts near the Bali Barat National Park, which offers the best diving in Bali around Menjangan Island. **Mimpi Resort Menjangan**, www.mimpiresorts.com For excellent diving with added 'feel-good' factor, go to **Pemutaran Village Resort** where coral reefs have been reconstructed and conserved. There are several hotels here, for instance the **Adi Assri Beach Cottages**, www.adiassri.com

WHERE TO EAT

Most hotels have restaurants, and in **Sanur** and **Nusa Dua** there are few good restaurants unattached to hotels. Even so, do try eating out of the hotel for more authentic cooking – and much lower prices. **Kuta** has an excellent range, like the long-established Poppies, tel: 0361 751 059 (Poppies Lane), while TJs serves top-quality Mexican food, tel: 0361 751 093. Kuta Puri, Poppies Gang 1, Kuta, tel: 0361 751 903, is typical of the best of the Kuta restaurants: superb cocktails, wonderful ambience, efficient service and tasty food. There are plenty of night-spots in Kuta/Legian: the **Skygarden** is good – try to get a spot on the top floor.
At Sanur, try **The Gangsa**, away from the main street at Jl Tirta

Akasa 28, tel: 0361 270 260, or **Kayu Manis**, Jl Tandakan 6, tel: 0361 289 410.
Ubud has good restaurants – choose the more expensive ones for the best quality food. **The Café Lotus**, in the centre of Ubud, has good food and décor – and a fine temple on the other side of the lotus pond. **Murni's Warung**, just before Campuhan bridge, has been serving excellent cakes and meals for years, tel: 0361 975 233. The **Dragonfly**, between Monkey Forest Road and Hanuman Road, offers good food. Most of the cafés and restaurants offer free Wi-Fi access.

SHOPPING

Bali has excellent shopping: a lot of designers work from here. For clothes head for Kuta, Seminyak and Ubud. For crafts, buy at source in the craft villages where possible. Visit the government-run **Sanggraha Kriya Asta Handicrafts Centre** in Denpasar (fixed prices, good quality) to get an idea of what the price should be elsewhere. If you have little time, Metis combines excellent eating with artisans' boutiques (Jl Petitenget, Seminyak, www.metisbali.com).
Ubud and surrounding villages are packed with art galleries, ranging from the catchpenny to the stylish. The huge **Agung Rai** complex in Peliatan is one of the best.
To find out what's on during your stay in Bali, visit www.bali.com

6
Nusa Tenggara

Drier, wilder and less fertile than Bali, the Nusa Tenggara islands – formerly known as the Lesser Sundas – are mountainous, sheltering villages and cultures cocooned against change by long years of inaccessibility. While cloves and nutmeg drew the colonial powers to Maluku, in the Lesser Sundas they came for the great stands of aromatic sandalwood on Sumba and Timor. The Portuguese had by the 16th century established missions in eastern Flores and the Alor and Solor islands, and continued to hold East Timor long after they lost control of Maluku.

The Dutch paid little attention to the area; not until the 20th century did they move to stamp out headhunting, human sacrifice and intertribal wars. Even then, with no obvious mineral wealth or precious spices, the islands were left almost untouched, particularly their inaccessible interiors. As a result they boast a stunning cultural inheritance.

It is not just the opportunity to observe unique cultures in mountain strongholds that draws visitors. Off the coasts, notably around Flores and Komodo, are fine coral reefs, while the 'dragons' of Komodo, the high peak of Gunung Rinjani, and the coloured lakes of Keli Mutu are the focus of national parks. Added mystique was sparked with the 2003 discovery, in a cave in Flores, of the bones of a tiny hominid thought to have lived on the islands up to 12,000 years ago. Scientific argument has raged as to whether the bones represent a completely new species – named *Homo floresiensis* – or merely members of *Homo sapiens* with congenital disorders.

Tourism throughout Nusa Tenggara is developing all the time, with good hotels, improving roads and excellent flight

CLIMATE

If you travel to Nusa Tenggara during the wet season, Nov–Jun, be prepared for torrential rains to cause flooding and wash away roads – at other times the land will be parched and dry. In some parts of Nusa Tenggara, notably Timor, there can be tropical cyclones. Aug and Sep are generally the driest months.

◀ *Opposite: Pulau Rakit, in Sumbawa's Saleh Bay.*

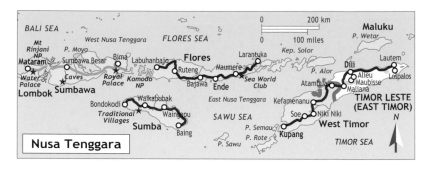

connections. Administratively, the area is divided into two provinces: the western islands are Nusa Tenggara Barat (NTB) and the eastern ones are Nusa Tenggara Timur (NTT). The eastern part of Timor Island became the independent country of Timor Leste (formerly East Timor) in 2002.

LOMBOK

Dominated by the huge, looming bulk of 3726m (12,225ft) Mt Rinjani, Lombok has a totally different feel to Bali, across the deep Lombok Straits. Lombok is less developed – especially in the south. Around a tenth of the population of 3 million are of Balinese Hindu descent, and you can find rice terraces as finely sculpted as in Bali, ornate Hindu temples and shrines and many Balinese rituals. But Lombok boasts its own special character and identity, not least because the form of Islam practised by its native Sasak people is a unique variant known as Waktu Telu – or Wetu Telu – influenced by both animism and Balinese Hinduism.

Ampenan, Mataram, Cakranegara

The four towns of Ampenan, Mataram, Cakranegara and Sweta have merged to form a single metropolis, hectic but worth a morning's exploration. At the mouth of the Jankok River, hundreds of outrigger canoes are lined up on the beach. Handmade pottery is on sale at the Lombok Pottery Centre on Jl Sriwijaya. The main market (look for weaving and pottery) is on the road heading north to Senggigi, while a little further on is Sudirman's Antiques, selling traditional crafts. The Pura Segara temple is a few minutes' walk. The

Chinese cemetery beyond has graves highly decorated with coloured porcelain. Many of the dead here were killed in the aftermath of the 1965 attempted coup. The Nusa Tenggara Barat Museum on Jl Panji Tilar Negara, in Mataram, is worth visiting. Cakranegara (known as Cakra) is the most rewarding area of the city. A craft and weaving centre, it also boasts two of the most important Balinese buildings on Lombok – the Mayura Water Palace and Pura Meru. Next door to the bus station at Sweta is a vast covered market – the largest and most comprehensive on Lombok.

Mayura Water Palace **

A peaceful oasis amid busy Cakra, the complex centres on a huge, rectangular pond almost covered with lotus flowers. In the middle is the floating palace, the Bale Kambang, a pavilion from which justice was administered in the 18th century. The palace was not always peaceful. In 1894 independence fighters here defeated and killed the Dutch General Van Hamm and his entire expeditionary force, which had camped in the palace grounds.

Meru Pura, Lombok's largest and most important Hindu temple, was built in 1720 by Balinese Prince Anak Agung Made Karang to unify the small Hindu kingdoms of Lombok. There are over 30 shrines here.

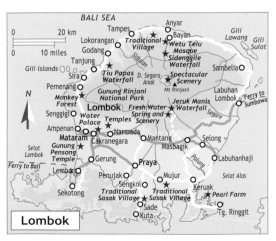

Lombok

FESTIVALS

Like their neighbours across the Lombok Straits, the Balinese of Lombok hold many temple festivals, notably around Cakra. The **Sasak** and **Wetu Telu** ceremonies are mainly in the months just before the rains come – Oct–Nov. If in the area, don't miss the **Nyale** (sea-worm) festival at Kuta, usually in the first or second week of Feb. At full moon ceremonies are often held around Anak Segara lake on Mt Rinjani. There are also spectacular festivities surrounding ceremonies such as circumcision or the opening of a new paddy field.

SENGGIGI BEACH

Thirty years ago a visit to Senggigi would have revealed a couple of reasonable hotels and a few guesthouses overlooking beautiful bays. Today there dozens of hotels. Nearby, **Batu Bolong** is a Balinese temple on a rocky point from which, it is said, virgins were thrown into the sea. The temple is named for the hole in the rock nearby (*batu* = 'stone', *bolong* = 'hole'). Spend the afternoon on the beach and then watch a technicolor sunset over Bali's Mt Agung. **Pura Segara**, another Balinese temple, is right on the beach to the south of Senggigi, beyond Batu Bolong.

NUSA TENGGARA

RINJANI NATIONAL PARK

Rinjani's good management was recognized in 2004 when it won a World Legacy Award. Tour operators and most hotels organize treks up Rinjani, as do guesthouses in Ampenan and Cakra. Most people start the trek from Sembalun Lawang village, although there are other entry points too, each with its own cooperative of guides and porters. The trek lasts four days and shouldn't be undertaken lightly – it's cold up there, and it's a tough climb to the top. From the crater rim you see Bali to the west, Sumbawa to the east. Climb down to the huge Anak Segara crater lake (2100m) and bathe your weary limbs in delicious hot springs, coloured milky by minerals. You are unlikely to have the place to yourself – especially at full moon, when both Balinese and Sasak come to make offerings to their ancestors at this sacred place. Find out more at www.lombok-network.com/rinjani

PHOTOGRAPHING TOMBS

In many villages you will be asked to make a donation to photograph tombs – the living are still paying for having buried the dead with honour.

From the Three Cities

Gunung Pengson is a small Balinese temple with stunning views on a rocky promontory south of Mataram. Visit early in the morning to see it at its best. Narmada, near Cakra, is the old summer palace of the Raja of Mataram. The lake here was created in 1805 in the shape of Mt Rinjani's Anak Segara lake when the Raja became too old and frail to climb Rinjani itself to make the proper offerings to the volcano's gods.

From Narmada drive to Lingsar, a large temple complex even older (1714) and holier than Pura Meru. Both Sasak Wetu Telu believers and Balinese Hindus worship here, at different shrines. The Waktu Telu shrine includes a spring inhabited by sacred black eels. The village holds an annual dance and music festival, using its important and ancient gamelan. Suranadi, a further 20min into the hills from Lingsar, is a quieter temple and pilgrimage site.

Gili Islands

On the tiny Gili Islands (*gili* means 'island' in the local language) the atmosphere is laid-back and hip. There are lovely beaches here. Gili Meno is the quietest of the three main islands and has the fewest tourist facilities. Gili Trawangan has the liveliest atmosphere, with nightly beach parties, and the best snorkelling. Gili Air, closest to Lombok, is busy and the most heavily populated. Fourth and quietest is Gili Nanggu near Lembar Harbour. There is good information at www.lombok-network.com/gili_islands/

North Lombok

From Pemenang (good market) head north to the stunning white sand beach at Sira, near which are several luxury hotels. There are small fishing villages and dreamy beaches all the way up the coast. From Gondang walk inland to see caves and the Tiu Papas waterfall; a short drive inland is the Wetu Telu village of Gangga. Double back to the coast and continue north to Anyer before reaching Bayan, one of the most important Watu Telu villages – Islam is said to have arrived on Lombok here, and it has the oldest mosque on the island. From Bayan visit Senaru and its spectacular waterfall of Sindang Gila, said to have healing powers.

South and Central Lombok

Less influenced by the Balinese, the south and centre of Lombok are the heartlands of the island's native Sasak culture. Regular day trips are organized by Senggigi hotels and tour operators, but it is more fun to hire a car or jeep. From the Three Cities take the Praya road. Before reaching busy Praya (good market) turn off to the village of Sukarara, where weavers use wooden backstrap looms to create fine pieces – some taking months to complete.

A few minutes south, take another turning off the main road to visit the pottery centre of Penujak. Other villages in the area also produce traditional pottery. Back on the main road, head south through Sengkol to Sade (also known as Rembitan), a traditional Sasak village where the government has stepped in to protect the traditional thatched houses and rice barns. It feels a bit like a living museum, but it gives a good idea of how people used to live.

From Sade it is a few minutes' drive to Kuta Beach, on the south coast. Still relatively quiet, it is the antithesis of its Balinese namesake and well worth an overnight stay. From Kuta turn inland via Batu Nampar, with its huge saltpans, making a detour to see the traditional village of Batu Rintang. Then go north through the craft village of Beleka to rejoin the main east–west highway at Kopang.

East Lombok

As you explore the less-visited east, watch for views of Mt Rinjani. North of Labuhan Lombok are fishing villages where foreigners are still a novelty. Offshore are the uninhabited islands of Gili Sulat, Gili Lampu and Gili Lawang, with excellent snorkelling over unspoiled coral reefs.

SUMBA

Western Sumba is most famous for its megaliths and death feasts; eastern Sumba has some of the finest *ikat* weaving in the world. Stylized patterns are used to make pictures of tribal history in vivid, glowing colours. You will see everywhere the small, sturdy horses used in traditional fights with small boys lovingly grooming them (*see* panel on the Pasola).

▲ *Above: Mt Rinjani, with the Anak Segara crater lake in the foreground.*

TRADITIONAL DANCE

While traditional dance features in festivals in country villages – notably Lingsar – it's usually easiest to see dances at performances arranged by tour operators and hotels. Dances include the *tari oncer* drum dance, *batek baris*, *telek* and the *gandrung* love-dance – frowned upon by orthodox Muslims. Trance dances are performed in Lombok (as in Java and Bali), but are rarely seen. Javanese *wayang sasak* puppet theatre and *wayang orang* performances are also staged.

NUSA TENGGARA

▶ Opposite: A view from Rinca, one of the island homes of the famous Komodo dragons.

Waingapu

Administrative capital of the island, the port makes a good centre from which to investigate *ikat* weaving. First go to Melolo, an hour's drive from Waingapu. Nearby are several weaving villages. Rende has big slab tombs. At Pau, which has retained its Raja, ask to see his collection of fabrics. There are more tombs, traditional houses and weaving at Umbara, and Baing is known for its scarves. At Kailala (just before Baing) the Kailala Beach Resort offers game fishing.

Western Sumba

Celebrated for its Pasola festival, western Sumba is also the place to see death rituals and feasts as spectacular and complex as any in Sulawesi's Toraja. Buffalo, horses and even dogs are slaughtered, and the deceased are buried with their favourite possessions and in rich fabrics they could not have afforded in life. The tomb is marked by massive stones – some weigh many tonnes and require the labour of hundreds to drag them into place. The neat little market town of Waikabubak is the obvious base to explore this area, which is cooler and greener than eastern Sumba.

Villages Near Waikabubak

Pasunga has superb tombs; one, erected in the mid-1920s, required the sacrifice of 150 water-buffaloes. At Anakalang there is a biannual mass marriage. Matakakeri has Sumba's heaviest tomb, at over 70 tonnes. Walk on to an all but deserted hilltop hamlet with yet more tombs. Sodan is the site of a lunar new year ceremony, and owns a drum covered in human skin. Prai Goli has some of Sumba's oldest megaliths.

SUMBAWA

Surfers have discovered Sumbawa's stunning beaches – notably Lakey Beach at Hu'u – and Moyo Island, now partly a game reserve, boasts one of the best hideaway luxury hotels in eastern Indonesia. In the forested hills around Sumbawa Besar are huge neolithic tombs, while the Dou Donggo people of the eastern Sumbawa mountains are known for their animist beliefs. Mt Tambora makes for a spectacular but tough climb (*see* panel).

Sumbawa Besar and Surrounds

Capital of western Sumbawa is Sumbawa Besar ('Big Sumbawa'), a sprawling, noisy Islamic trading centre. The Dalem Loka (Sultan's palace built in 1885) is worth seeing, although in poor condition. Moyo Island, with its beautiful coral reefs, is easily reached by boat from Sumbawa Besar. Batu Tering (30min drive) has interesting megaliths and stone carvings. Hire a guide to see 2000-year-old carved sarcophagi.

Bima

Capital of the eastern portion of Sumbawa, Bima lies in a staunchly Islamic area and was formerly an important trading centre. Local women weave colourful chequered textiles unlike any others in Indonesia.

KOMODO ★★★

Protected by some of the most dangerous waters in Indonesia, the monstrous Komodo dragon (*Varanus komodoensis*), the world's biggest lizard, is found only on the islands of Komodo and Rinca. It was formally identified in 1910. An adult can measure over 3m (10ft) long and weigh over 130kg (290lb), and comes equipped with huge claws and sharp teeth. The dragons hunt deer, wild boar and ponies. They lie in wait, their grey-beige hide perfectly camouflaged by the dry scrub, then lash out at their victim with their muscular tail or sharp teeth. Animals which escape an initial attack seldom survive – the dragon's saliva quickly induces blood poisoning.

Accommodation on the island is in lodges at the rangers' camp in a huge and beautiful bay – although the majority of tourists sleep aboard their cruise ships or make day-trips from Labuan Bajo, on Flores. You will have no difficulty in seeing Komodo dragons around the camp or on ranger-led trips into the bush. Rinca is also a good place to see them, and with fewer tourists. Keep a careful eye open as you look around: the dragons are quite common, but when they sit absolutely motionless they are very hard to spot. In addition to dragon-watching, you can

relax by snorkelling on the reefs in the national park. There are fantastic coral formations and an amazing variety of fish, but take local advice, as the currents are extremely strong. The reefs around Komodo are known by serious divers as amongst the best in Indonesia – which means the best in the world. There are several dive companies in Labuan Bajo offering live-aboard, week-long trips or just day-cruises.

FLORES

Named Cabo dos Flores – 'Cape of Flowers' – after the underwater coral gardens by 16th-century Portuguese sandalwood traders, Flores is the most spectacular island in eastern Nusa Tenggara, with its mountainous scenery. The cultures and traditions of Flores' five distinct tribal groups are as varied and interesting as the island's scenery.

Labuan Bajo

Once a tiny fishing village and ferry port, Labuan Bajo is mushrooming into one of Indonesia's most hip destinations. Hotels and restaurants are stacked up the steep hillside overlooking the bay, and the beaches are fast becoming lined with more. It is still pleasant and relaxed, with the strongly Islamic local feel tempered by incomers from all over the archipelago and further afield. Use the town as your base for exploring Komodo National Park, while inland are some fascinating tours to traditional villages and into the hills.

Ruteng

Capital of the Manggarai people, this town is set high on a hillside below an active volcano. The area is famous for *caci* whip-fighting duels. Blood spilled is considered an offering

to the ancestor spirits. Duels are a feature of weddings and important ceremonies and a high point of Independence Day (17 Aug) celebrations. Few of Manggarai's traditional round houses survive, although there are some in Todo, half an hour's drive from Ruteng. The textiles here have brightly coloured patterns embroidered on a black or dark blue background. If you fly over Ruteng, look down

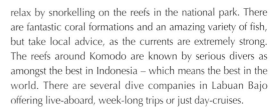

FEEDING THE DRAGONS

After years of feeding dragons a slaughtered goat when tourists arrived, the authorities now force them to forage for themselves, giving tourists the opportunity of seeing them in more natural surroundings.

CRUISING

Most ship-based tourists only spend a couple of hours on Komodo, but it is rewarding to spend at least a night here and go into the bush when there are fewer people around. Take a ranger – the dragons are dangerous.

from the plane to spot the traditional land-ownership pattern of pie-slice wedges radiating out from a hill-top: that way, everyone got their fair share of hilly and flatter land.

Riung *

This port has an island-studded bay and dazzling reefs. Huge monitor lizards (some almost as large as Komodo dragons) are found in the area, and at dusk the sky is darkened by flocks of huge fruit bats. The diving and snorkelling industry is just getting off the ground, with one or two good places to stay which can also organize visits to the offshore islands.

Bajawa and Surrounds

Ngadhu and *bhaga* structures stand in the squares of the many villages surrounding Bajawa. The *ngadhu* is a carved wooden pole with a rough thatched roof, and symbolizes the male ancestors; the female line is shown in the *bhaga*, a miniature thatched house representing the womb. Bena is the best known and best preserved of all the traditional villages in the area. Langa, on the road to Bena, has more *ngadhu* and *bhaga* and some fine weaving. A 20-minute walk towards the rockstrewn slopes of Mt Inieri is a spectacular rift valley. Soa, about 30–40min from Bajawa, is built around a huge, natural amphitheatre with tiers of megaliths.

Moni and Surrounds

Moni is beautifully set in a high valley. Most visitors arrive, stay overnight, see Keli Mutu and then go, but the area is worth a couple of days. Wolowaru has traditional houses with shaggy, palm-thatched roofs and, inside, carvings. The three most famous weaving villages, Ngella, Wolojita and Jopu, can be visited on foot from Wolowaru in a long day.

Mt Keli Mutu ***

High above Moni, the three crater lakes of Keli Mutu are special: each is a different colour, and the colours change from time to time. The two largest are separated by a narrow, rocky spine. The colours in these two are paler than in the third, with yellows, whites, blues, greens and turquoise predominating. The third, 200m (220yd) away, ranges from oily

A TERRIFYING RIDE?

Travelling west from Moni to Ende, vertigo sufferers and those of a nervous disposition should sit on the right of the bus. Winding through a spectacular narrow gorge subject to landslides and rockfalls, the road is so narrow that the bus's wheels are almost on the edge of the ravine.

◀ *Opposite: Komodo dragons move sleepily – but can put on a terrific turn of speed when hunting.*
▼ *Below: The waterfront at Maumere.*

dark green to blood-red and even black. Most people visit for sunrise and leave straight afterwards, but if you stay around you'll find the sun brings out the colours more brilliantly – and you'll have the place to yourself.

Maumere and Surrounds

Maumere is the largest town on Flores and a stopover on the popular overland route. It has several pretty and relaxed beaches nearby and some reasonable diving. Ladalero, a Catholic seminary high in the hills above Maumere, has wonderful panoramic views of the bay beyond and an interesting museum. On the south coast (40 minutes' drive), Sikka is probably eastern Flores' best weaving centre.

Larantuka

The little port of Larantuka nestles under the flank of the active Ili Mandiri volcano. On Good Friday the people of Larantuka parade a statue of Our Lady through the town, led by a religious order known as the Konfrerie. Accompanying songs are in Latin and archaic Portuguese – both now incomprehensible to the people. Alor, Pantar and other tiny islands are accessible by plane or ferry from here – visit them to feel truly remote and for some fabulous diving.

TIMOR

In the more remote hill villages of Timor, people still live in beehive-shaped houses with thatched roofs reaching almost to the ground. Throughout the island you can find heavy woven fabrics featuring geckos, crocodiles and stylized human figures, often in very dramatic colours.

Kupang

Kupang, the main town in West Timor and the provincial capital, is a gateway to Nusa Tenggara and an important entry point from Australia (via Darwin). Visit Teddy's Bar on the waterfront for tours, information and good food.

The regional museum (Museum Negeri) is on Jl Perintis Kemerdekaan. At Oebelo (20 minutes' drive) villagers make and sell traditional stringed instruments. The Savu *ikat* weavers' co-operative (Yasayan le Rai) on Jl Hati Suci is a

BUYING *IKAT* AND OTHER LOCAL CLOTHS

Genuine hand-woven cloths are narrow – the width of a backstrap loom. Local sarongs consist of two narrow lengths sewn together. Natural dyes are sometimes still used, but chemicals are more frequent, occasionally in the earthy colours of natural ones. Cheaper factory-made cloths have the design printed on rather than woven in – it will be more apparent on one side of the fabric than the other. On Flores the colours used in Nggela, Jopu and other villages near Ende tend to be reds and earthy browns – quite unlike the dark blues favoured around Maumere and Ruteng and the richer reds of Sikka. Because many weavers in the Ende region are Muslim, patterns are often abstract; in the mainly Christian villages Nggela, Jopu and Wolojita, animals, people and even ships feature.

craft outlet for weavers on remote Savu Island. Weaving can be seen also at Dharma Bakti's factory near the harbour (arrange a visit at their shop at Jl Sumba 32). Oesao (30min) saw fierce fighting between the Japanese and Australians in 1942, and has a good daily market. There are good beaches (avoid weekends) around the bay. Try Laisana Beach or take a day trip to Semau or Monkey Island. Both have good snorkelling, and there are a couple of small hotels on Semau.

From Kupang

Take the interesting, winding road to Soe (2–3 hours), a cool, dry hill town with a good market and adequate hotels. Hire a car to visit small towns and traditional villages such as Boti or Kapan. To the east of Niki Niki (30min) is spectacular countryside with huge rocks (*fatukopa*) said to be a gathering point for the souls of the dead. Atambua is midway between Kupang (7 hours) and Dili in East Timor (6 hours); don't miss the town market for fabrics and jewellery and to meet traditional country people. Another fascinating trip is the the island of Rote, off the south-western tip of Timor. The island has been known to surfers for several years, but others can enjoy the tranquillity and the intricate weaving: and you can be certain that the villagers see few tourists.

TIMOR LESTE

The eastern part of Timor is the independent country of Timor Leste, occupied by Indonesia from 1976 to 1999. It is popular with tourists needing to leave and re-enter Indonesia at the end of the one-month visa period, but it's important to check the security situation before you stay longer.

Dili, the capital, is an attractive town with old Portuguese buildings and wide, tree-lined avenues. A huge statue of Christ (built in 1996) stands atop a hill near the city, reached by a pleasantly undemanding walk and giving beautiful views, especially at sunset. The hill towns of Maubisse and Aileu are centres of coffee-growing – the country's main industry – while around Los Palos are cave paintings and stone sarcophagi. There are wonderful beaches and islands, especially Jaco Island, and people are friendly to foreigners. There is little good accommodation outside Dili.

◄ *Opposite: One of the enchanting traditional dwellings on Flores.*

HAVEN

An early Western visitor to Kupang was Captain William Bligh, who put in here in 1789 after travelling 6500km (4000 miles) in an open boat since being cast adrift by the *Bounty* mutineers.

ALOR AND PANTAR ARCHIPELAGO

Wild and mountainous, the islands to the east of Flores have barely been affected by the 20th century, let alone the 21st. Animist beliefs, such as the *naga* snake cult persist. Traditional villages drowse beneath smoking volcanoes and fishermen dive for pearls on pristine reefs. The whaling village of **Lamalera** on **Lembata (Lomblen) Island** is the greatest attraction, and on neighbouring **Alor Island** you can see ancient bronze Moko drums whose origins remain a mystery.

GETTING THERE AND AROUND

Cruising: Cruise ships are the most comfortable way to visit and often stop at remote places which are almost impossible to visit any other way.

By air: There is a good network of airports. The three hubs are Denpasar, Bima and Kupang, from where small planes radiate out to remote islands.

By road: Road travel tends to be bumpy. Cars with drivers can be hired in most places.

By sea: Ferries connect the islands. Check locally for up-to-date schedules.

WHERE TO STAY

Outside of Lombok, there are an increasing number of dive resorts dotted about the Nusa Tenggara archipelago, many catering to general interest tourists too. They are often the most comfortable and peaceful places to stay.

Lombok
LUXURY
Senggigi Beach Hotel, tel: 0370 693 210, www.senggigi beachhotel.com Includes a selection of luxury villas.
Alang-Alang Boutique Beach Hotel, Jl Raya Mangsit Senggigi, tel: 0370 693 518, www.alang-alang-villas.com

MID-RANGE
Puri Mas Boutique Resort & Spa, Jl Raya, Mangsit Beach, tel: 0370 693831, www.purimas-lombok.com
Windy Beach Cottages, Pantai Mangsit, tel: 0370 693 191, www.windy-beach.com

The Gilis
There are dozens of guest-houses on the three main islands. Several dive operators have joined forces to foster reef conservation and run a turtle conservation project. On Gili Trawangan, try the charming **Desa Dunia Beda**, tel: 0370 641 575, www.desaduniabeda.com

Narmada
Suranadi Hotel, tel: 0370 633 686, www.suranadihotel.com In the hills near the temple.

Kuta Beach
Novotel Lombok, Mandalika Resort, tel: 0370 653 333, www.novotellombok.com This is the best, and there are many other smaller hotels.

Sumba
Nihiwatu Resort, www.nihiwatu.com An award-winning activity resort with a strong social conscience. Less expensive and closer to the airport is **Newa Sumba Resort**, www.newasumbaresort.com Also in the southwest is the **Sumba Nautil Resort**, www.sumbanautilresort.com In Waingapu, the capital, the **Hotel Elvin** has recently been renovated: Jl A. Yani 73, tel: 0387 61462.

Waikabubak
Hotel Manandang, Jl Pemuda 4, tel: 0387 21297.

Sumbawa
The **Amanwana**, Moyo Island, tel: 0371 22330, www.amanresorts.com Luxury hideaway.

Sumbawa Besar
Tambora, Jl Kebayan, tel: 0371 21555.
Tirtasari Cottages, tel: 0371 21987, 5km (3 miles) out of the town; good restaurant.

Flores
Larantuka
Hotel Fortuna, Jl Diponegoro, just out of town.
Hotel Rulies, the backpackers' choice – friendly and clean.

Alor
Alor Dive Resort, tel: 0813 1780 4133, www.alor-divers.com

Maumere
Sao Wisata Dive Resort, Jl Sawista, Waiara, tel: 0382 21555, www.saowisata.com
Sea World Club, Maumere 861181, tel: 0382 21570, www.sea-world-club.com

Moni
Not much choice here, but the **Sao Ria Wisata** is the most comfortable option. The **Wisma St Franciskus**, at Detusoko, is plain and clean.

Bajawa
Hotel Happy Happy is new and the most comfortable: Jl Sudirman, tel: 0384 21763, www.hotelhappyhappy.com
Villa Silverin is a good place for an overnight stay, but it's a bit far from the town.

Ruteng
The Catholic Mission offers clean rooms and hot showers, and is by far the most popular

place to stay – known locally as the **Hotel Susteran**.

Riung
Nirvana Bungalows, Jl Pelabuhan, tel: 081 337 106007, www.mymeeshmeesh.wix.com/nirvanabungalows

Labuhanbajo
Green Hill Hotel, Jl Soekarno-Hatta, tel: 0385 41289, www.greenhillboutiquehotel.com Centrally located with lovely views over the bay. Away from the bustle of the town, the **Bajo Komodo Ecolodge** is part of an eco-friendly group; tel: 0385 41391, www.ecolodgesindonesia.com/bajo There are several hotels on islands a short ride from the mainland: most luxurious is **Angel Island Resort**, on Bidadari Island, tel: 0385 41443, www.angelisleflores.com **Seraya Bungalows**, on Seraya Island, is a good alternative: tel/fax: 0385 41258, www.serayaisland.com

Kupang
Hotel Astiti, Jl Sudirman 166, tel: 0380 830622, www.astitihotel.wordpress.com/2009/12/13/hotel-astiti-kupang/
Swiss-Belinn Kristal Kupang, Jl Timur Raya 59, tel: 0391 825 100, www.swiss-belhotel.com/en/Indonesia/Kupang/kupang#hotel+information Has a pool and is on the beach.

Timor Leste (Dili)
More and more hotels are opening here as the country establishes itself.

Hotel Esplanada is centrally located with views over the bay; tel: 0670 3313 088, www.hotelesplanada.com **Pousada Casa do Sandalo** is getting good reviews; tel: 0670 331 0409.

SHOPPING

Lombok
Many Balinese souvenirs are made here because labour costs are lower, but there are genuine local crafts too. Look for bamboo and wooden containers, palm-leaf boxes, accessories for betel-chewing, beautiful rough earthenware pottery, rattan basketry, brightly coloured sarongs and scarves (some using *ikat* techniques), musical instruments and replicas of wooden horses used in Sasak ritual dances. In the weaving cooperatives of **Cakranegara** buy fantastic heavy silk or cotton curtaining and upholstery fabrics. Out of town, for weaving try **Sukarara**, **Sengkol**, **Sade** or **Pringgasela** (in east Lombok). **Senanti** and **Sukaraja** specialize in woodcarvings, while **Penujak**, **Banyumuluk** and **Masbagik** are good for pottery. At **Gunung Sari** craftsmen busily make 'antiques' for the art shops.

Sumba
No problem buying wonderful double-*ikat* weave fabrics – only in repelling enthusiastic salesmen! Read up in advance about what to look for if you are a serious collector – or, as ever, just buy what you like.

Flores
Larantuka
Pearls, woven fabrics; look for old Chinese vases, ceramics.

Maumere
Look for beautiful lengths of cloth in the villages or in the market.

Timor
Ikat weavings from all over Nusa Tenggara, sandalwood carvings, betel-nut containers, and weaving/hats made from lontar palm leaves.

DIVING

There are dive operators based in several locations throughout Nusa Tenggara. There are also operators running live-aboard dive cruises from Bali. Try:
Aquamarine Diving – Bali: www.aquamarinediving.com
Dive Komodo – Labuan Bajo: www.divekomodo.com

LOMBOK	J	F	M	A	M	J	J	A	S	O	N	D
AVERAGE TEMP. °F	82	82	82	80	80	82	78	78	80	82	82	82
AVERAGE TEMP. °C	28	28	28	27	27	28	26	26	27	28	28	28
RAINFALL in	19	11	6	4	2	3	3	1	1	2	5	10
RAINFALL mm	494	273	148	104	61	73	75	27	18	44	128	245
DAYS OF RAINFALL	22	19	11	8	6	8	4	3	4	4	11	19

7
Sulawesi

The main attractions in Sulawesi are the culture of the **Torajan highlanders** in South Sulawesi and the glorious reefs and well-organized diving of the Bunaken Marine National Park in the north and the Wakatobi islands in the southeast. But Sulawesi has much more to offer, from the boat-building villages of the southern peninsula to the hunter-gatherer tribes of the centre. Throughout this fascinating, orchid-shaped island are mountain ranges, volcanoes, fantastic beaches, waterfalls and thick forests sheltering unique wildlife. The road network has improved and inter-island flights make exploration easier, but be prepared for long distances and arduous conditions if you are travelling beyond the main tourist places, especially in the mountainous spine and centre of the island.

To the far north are the lands of the **Minahasa**, where Christianity took root with the arrival of the Portuguese. A volcanic region, the north boasts stunning coral reefs, colourful dance ceremonies and ancient graves.

Further south, in **Central Sulawesi**, are megaliths, stone statues and huge vats, and the **Lore Lindu National Park**, a mecca for bird-watchers. The southwestern peninsula is dominated by the **Bugis** people, the seafarers who so terrified Western sailors that they inspired the word 'bogeyman'. Traditional Buginese ships – *pinisi* – are still constructed in villages along the coast. 4th- and 5th-century Buddhist images have been found in **South Sulawesi**, evidencing the long centuries of trade the Buginese have engaged in, while Ming and Sung dynasty funerary wares are still occasionally uncovered by archaeologists – and grave-robbers.

CLIMATE

It is rainier in southern Sulawesi than in the north, with microclimates depending on the topography. The Palu valley, in Central Sulawesi, has the lowest rainfall in Indonesia.

◄ *Opposite: The lavishly decorated architecture tells you that you are in Sulawesi's Torajaland.*

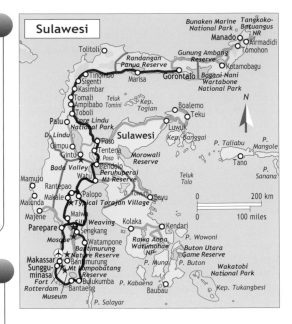

▼ *Below: Benteng Ujung Pandang, called by its Dutch builders Fort Rotterdam.*

SOUTH SULAWESI

Gateway to Sulawesi – indeed, to eastern Indonesia – is **Makassar**, where the hair-oil that forced the use of protective antimacassars on 19th-century chairs and sofas was made. The city is hot, frenetic and noisy, but has its charms, particularly around the old port area.

The best-preserved ancient fort in Indonesia is **Fort Rotterdam** (Benteng Ujung Pandang). Within the ramparts are two museums, a music and dance conservatory (you can watch rehearsals) and an archaeological institute.

A ride by *becak* through back streets from a Conrad novel will take you to **Paotere Harbour** to see Buginese schooners or *pinisi,* still with masts and sails but now with engines to help them along. The **Clara Bundt Orchid Garden** (Jl Mochtar Lufti 15) has some orchids for sale and a great shell collection. Hunt out gold and antique shops in **Jl Somba Opu** – some of which stock early Chinese porcelain (although at high prices). Many of these are attractive fakes, which you may not mind – but you need to know what you are looking for.

Around Makassar

See traditional boatbuilding in villages like **Bantaeng** and **Bulukumba**. At Bira Beach traditional schooners are overhauled and there are good diving facilities. **Bantimurung**, near the airport, is a national park with dramatic karst limestone scenery, waterfalls and huge, beautiful butterflies. Make a combined visit to Bantimurung and **Leang Leang**, which has cave-paintings thousands of years old. There are further caves around **Camba**, a pleasant hill town. **Sungguminasa** – 20–30 minutes south of Makassar – is the site of a former royal palace, now the Ballalompoa Museum housing a huge gold crown, weapons, costumes and other exhibits. Further south – about 5 hours' drive from Makassar – is one of Indonesia's hottest new destinations, Tanjung Bira. There's already a good variety of hotels here, from top-class to backpacker hostels, and there are pure white sand beaches and some great diving.

Southeast Sulawesi

The main draw of Sulawesi's southeastern leg is the Wakatobi Marine National Park, made up of several islands. Thanks to the UK-based conservation charity, Operation Wallacea, opening this area up to tourism, there are now good facilities for visitors to be able to enjoy the kaleidoscopic marine life. En route, visit traditional towns and villages such as Buton and Liya Toga.

Tanah Toraja ★★★

Tanah Toraja ('Land of the Toraja') is one of Indonesia's most popular destinations for cultural tours. You can fly in and out of Torajaland from Makassar to avoid the six-hour drive, but it's better to fly one way and drive the other to see the panoramic

▼ *Below: Rice paddies in Torajaland.*

▲ *Above: Sigunta village in Torajaland.*

WALKS AROUND TORAJA

Trekking in Toraja is excellent, partly because of the cooler climate. There are dozens of short walks around the villages and burial sites; a longer walk (four hours) is from Batutumonga in the hills above Rantepao, downhill all the way to Sadan (or even Rantepao) past traditional houses and cliff graves.

AT THE MARKET

The market takes place in Rantepao every six days. You may be charged a fee to get in, but it is worth it for the dozens of stalls selling all manner of local goods, food and domestic animals – don't miss the pig market! You may even catch a cock-fight. The long bamboo containers hold fermented sugar-palm sap or rice wine – delicious early in the morning, but sour later.

mountain scenery. Tourism has brought prosperity, but development has not marred the beauty of the green river valleys and vast sweeps of rice terraces beneath rocky mountain ridges.

The traditional homes of the Toraja people, *tongkonan*, cluster behind huge stands of bamboo. Houses and rice-barns have upturned roofs like a ship. The walls are beautifully carved and painted with red, yellow, black and white clan motifs. Water-buffalo skulls and horns indicate past ceremonies.

The Dutch won control of Toraja early in the 20th century by bringing warring tribes down from the hills and outlawing human sacrifice. Missionaries soon followed and the area is now mainly Christian but, as in many parts of Indonesia, traditional beliefs in an afterworld and ancestor-reverence persist.

These beliefs are at their most spectacular in the Torajan Festival of the Dead. Festivals can take years to organize as the dead cannot be consigned to the afterlife until their earthly inheritance is settled between family members – and disputes are common. Before the funeral the body remains at home (wrapped in funeral cloths) and the deceased is not considered to have fully passed on to the next world. The full ceremony takes up to a week. Even a relatively small event may involve killing 30–40 pigs (the meat is distributed around the village) and a half-dozen water-buffalo. The government now taxes animal offerings and places restrictions on expenditure as events were becoming more and more elaborate. Guests, including tourists, are welcome to attend.

The highlight is the funeral feast, involving animal slaughter (not for the squeamish!). The ceremony culminates in the body being taken to a cliff grave where the soul joins the ancestral spirits. Wealthy families commission a *tau tau*, a wooden statue of the dead person to which their soul can return, and these stare out eerily from balconies on the cliffs above the graves.

Most visitors stay in **Rantepao**, in the beautiful Sadan River valley. The district capital, **Makale**, a 20-minute drive away, is quieter but less convenient. The area is easy to get around – major sites of interest are signposted – and there are traditional houses, barns and burial sites everywhere. Walk away from paved roads to see less visited villages.

WEST SULAWESI

The province of West Sulawesi offers rough roads, small towns tourists never visit, and a Christianized culture similar to Toraja. A three-day hike through the mountains from Mamasa, staying in family homes or small guesthouses, brings you to Toraja – an amazing way to get there.

CENTRAL SULAWESI

Fly into Palu, then travel by road to Kamarora, where the headquarters of the Lore Lindu National Park are located. There is good bird-watching here and some interesting trekking deeper into the park – not too challenging and along good paths. For more adventure, use a combination of jeeps and trekking to visit the Bada Valley, to see the mysterious megalithic statues and then a further day's walk to the Besoa Valley, where there are huge stone vats, whose original purpose is unknown. There is simple accommodation at Kamarora, Gintu and Doda.

The area around Poso and Tentena is opening up again after some years of religious tension. It's a wonderful region of forests and mountains and huge Lake Poso. Tentena, at the northern end of the lake, is the starting point for treks and adventures; nearby is the magnificent Saluopa Waterfall.

WALLACEA

Sulawesi forms part of the biogeographical zone called Wallacea, marking the transition between the fauna and flora of Asia and of Australia. Much of the wildlife is unique to the island, e.g. the anoa, a dwarf buffalo, and the babirusa, like a pig but no relation. There is an astonishing variety of huge butterflies, and bird-watchers flock to view Sulawesi's high number of endemic species.

NORTHERN SULAWESI

The provinces of North Sulawesi are one of Indonesia's finest areas for general touring because of the well-surfaced roads, pretty villages, varied scenery and attractions, and friendly people. You can trek in wildlife reserves, see crater lakes and bubbling mudpits, and visit interesting archaeological sites – all surrounded by exquisite scenery. The Minahasa people are among the most prosperous in Indonesia and most are Christian.

Gorontalo is the best access point for the Togian Islands, a jewel-like scatter across the Gulf of Tomini. Excellent diving here and some fascinating sights: ask to see the diving goats! There are several dive resorts and 'away from it all' retreats.

▼ Below: An ancient megalith in Central Sulawesi.

SULAWESI

▲ Above: A Sulawesan pre-Christian tomb, or waruga.

AWAY FROM IT ALL

There is fabulous diving in the Wakatobi Marine National Park, in southeastern Sulawesi, and several remote islands where you can enjoy a conservation holiday.

TROPICAL NIGHTLIFE

Make sure visits to national parks or nature reserves include an overnight stay: tropical wildlife is most active in the early morning and late afternoon. Accommodation may be basic, but it is worth the discomfort to hear a tropical dawn chorus!

LOCAL DELICACIES

Minahasa cooking has some unusual specialities. Fruit bat is bony; dog is hot; rat (forest, not sewer) is delicious, a little like quail.

Manado and Surrounds

Capital of North Sulawesi, Manado is a bustling, efficient seaside city. **Bunaken Marine National Park** is the main draw. A 30-minute boat ride from the mainland are white sand beaches and well protected coral reefs with superlative snorkelling and diving. In the city, check out the **Provincial Museum** (Jl Supratman). Horse- and bullcart-races are occasionally held at **Ranomuut racetrack** east of the city.

Tomohon, a blissfully cool hill town with an interesting market, is a good base for exploring the region. The North Sulawesi peninsula is where two tectonic plates meet, so there is plenty of volcanic activity. **Mount Lokon** is a two-hour climb (easy but hot) from Wailan on the Manado–Tomohon road. The crater lake boils away when activity increases, and occasionally the mountain is 'closed' because of eruptions. A 20-minute drive from Tomohon is **Lake Linau**, a crater lake that changes colour according to the light. There are mud pools and small geysers: stick to the paths or risk being casseroled!

In pre-Christian times people here buried their dead in upright tombs, *warugas*. There are fine examples at **Airmadidi, Sawangan** and **Likupang**, many adorned with carvings revealing how the occupant died. **Batu Pinabetengan** is a huge stone marking the former meeting place of Minahasan chiefs.

Tara Tara village, close to Tomohon, is a centre of Minahasa culture where dance performances are sometimes held. Ask about the *cakalele* war dances, with dancers wearing Portuguese-style helmets and brightly coloured clothes.

Tangkoko Batuangus Nature Reserve

This pleasant reserve (two hours from Manado) is one of the best places to see Sulawesi's elusive wildlife. Tailless Celebes apes, hornbills and tiny tarsiers are frequently seen, while the megapode, which buries its eggs for hatching in the hot volcanic sands, takes more persistence to spot. There are black sand beaches and some good lowland forest. Overnight accommodation is in guesthouses. Tours can be arranged in Manado or Bitung.

GETTING THERE AND AROUND

By air: Makassar is the main gateway to Sulawesi with onward flights to other cities.

By road: Roads on the island are improving, but the heavy rain takes an annual toll.

WHERE TO STAY

Makassar
Singgasana Hotel, Jl Kajaolaliddo 6, tel: 0411 362 7051, www.makassar.singgasanahotels.com
Aston Makassar, Jl Sultan Hasanuddin, tel: 0411 362 3222, www.aston-international.com Both these hotels are centrally located and offer international standard rooms and facilities. Less expensive are the **Santika Makassar**, Jl Hasanuddin, tel: 0411 332 233, www.santika.com/makassar and the **Citra Wisata**, Jl Botolempangan, tel: 0411 311 018. For a touch of authenticity, stay at the home of Mursalim Dodo – the **Pen Man of Makassar**, donow77@hotmail.com

Tanjung Bira
Amatoa Resort, tel. 0813 5337 6865, www.amatoaresort.com Built on a cliff, with direct entry (by jumping!) into the clear sea. Less expensive and also good is **Salassa Guesthouse**, tel. 081 2426 5672.

Toraja
Toraja Heritage Hotel, Jl Kete Kesu, Rantepao, tel: 0423 21192; **Luta Resort Toraja**, Jl Dr Ratulangi 26, Rantepao, tel: 0423 21060; **Toraja Misiliana Hotel**, Jl Pong Tiku 27, tel: 0423 21212. South of Rantepao is the **Kandora Mountain Lodge**,

simple and adventurous but an ideal base for trekking; tel: 0423 21701, kandora@toraja.net

Palu
Swiss Bel-hotel Silae, Jl Malonda, tel: 0451 461 888, www.palu.swiss-belhotel.com
Hotel Santika, Jl Moh. Hatta 18, tel: 0451 424 888, www.santika.com

Tentena
Tando Bone Resort is a peaceful place on the western shore of Lake Poso; tel: 0458 21322, www.tandobone.net In Tentena, **Hotel Victoria** is clean and quiet.

Manado
There are several international chain hotels here, including: **Swiss-Belhotel Maleosan**, tel: 0431 861 000, www.manado.swiss-bellhotel.com and **Novotel Manado**, Jl Sam Ratulangi 22A, tel: 0431 55555, fax: 0431 63545. An hour from Manado, the **Highland Resort Tomohon** offers spa treatments and a peaceful stay in the hills; tel: 0431 353 333, www.highlandresort.info

Bunaken Dive Resorts
Amongst the best places to stay are the **Living Colours Dive Resort**, tel: 0812 430 6401, www.livingcoloursdiving.com

and the **Lumba Lumba Resort**, www.lumbalumbadiving.com

Togian Islands
There are several resorts, including **Poya Lisa Cottages**, just off Bomba Island, and **Black Marlin Resort**, tel: 0865 5720 2004, www.blackmarlindiving.com

Southeast Sulawesi
Wakatobi Resort, Kuta Poleng Blok D-1, Jl Setiabudi, Simpang Siur, Kuta, Bali, tel: 0361 759 669, www.wakatobi.com
Patuno Resort, tel: 0811 400 2221, www.patunoresort wakatobi.com

EATING AND SHOPPING

The seafood in Makassar is excellent, arguably the best in Indonesia. Try grilled fish (*ikan bakar*), crab (*kepiting*) and giant prawns (*udang*). The best crafts are sold in **Makassar** and **Rantepao**. Jl Somba Opu has shops with silver filigree jewellery from Kendari in Southeast Sulawesi and local gold. You can also hunt for brightly coloured silk sarongs, Chinese ceramics and local brasswork. In **Toraja**, buy painted and carved woodwork: boxes, bamboo water-carriers and machetes with bone-inlaid ebony handles.

MAKASSAR	J	F	M	A	M	J	J	A	S	O	N	D
AVERAGE TEMP. °F	78	78	78	78	78	78	78	78	80	80	80	78
AVERAGE TEMP. °C	26	26	26	26	26	26	26	26	27	27	27	26
RAINFALL in	28	20	15	8	5	2	2	1	1	2	12	22
RAINFALL mm	711	520	375	201	126	57	43	10	29	59	308	566
DAYS OF RAINFALL	25	23	21	18	15	10	7	3	5	9	20	23

8
Maluku

For hundreds of years the world's only source of nutmeg, mace and cloves, the islands of Maluku (the Moluccas) played a formative role in the history of empire-building by European nations. In the centre of the archipelago are the **Bandas**, tiny volcanic islands where nutmeg and its associated mace (the reddish fibres covering the nut) originated. In the north the islands of **Ternate**, **Tidore**, **Bacan** and **Halmahera** are the ancestral home of all the world's clove trees.

For centuries the route to the Spice Islands was guarded by Arab traders. The first Europeans to discover it were the Portuguese, who sent an expedition to Banda in 1512. The Spanish arrived – with Magellan – a decade later, followed soon after by the English and Dutch.

In the early 17th century the Dutch won control of the islands through one of history's most powerful mercantile organizations, the **Dutch East Indies Company** (VOC). Having captured Portuguese forts in **Ambon** and won control of the island, the VOC murdered competing English merchants. Then in 1621 VOC Governor General Jan Pieterszoon Coen seized control of the Bandas and the nutmeg monopoly. Within weeks about 15,000 Bandanese had been slaughtered. The English were ejected from their last stronghold, the island of **Run** – and compensated with an insignificant swampy island off the coast of New England, subsequently named Manhattan.

By now Coen and his lieutenants also had effective control of Ternate and Tidore. The cultivation and sale of cloves on these islands was banned, to centralize

CLIMATE

The rainy season in Ambon and southern Maluku is from April to August – the opposite to most of Indonesia – so the best months to visit are between October and January. Rain patterns in northern Maluku are like those of the rest of Indonesia.

◀ *Opposite: Begun in 1611 by the Dutch, Bandaneira's huge Fort Belgica has survived the test of time – and several major earthquakes.*

*** **The Kedaton in Ternate**:
partly open to visitors, partly
the splendid home of the
Sultan of Ternate.
** **Danau Laguna**: a beautiful
lagoon said to be the home
of a sacred crocodile.
*** **Bandaneira**: Don't miss
the chance to visit this
charming little town, once
the Dutch administrative
centre for the region.
Peaceful islands are home to
historic remains and wonderful coral reefs just offshore.

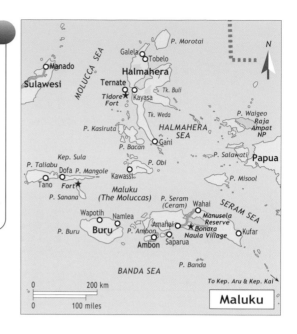

Maluku

production on Ambon and ensure a monopoly. Eventually,
however, clove and nutmeg seedlings were smuggled out,
breaking the monopoly and contributing to the demise of
the VOC.

Nutmeg and cloves are still harvested here, but it is the
islands' stunning natural beauty, world-class diving and
turbulent history that draw travellers. History is there to be
stumbled over. Innumerable forts crumble under the
grip of vines and banyan trees, and cannon em-
bossed with the VOC emblem slowly rust under the
tropical sun. The **Aru** archipelago is famous for its
birds-of-paradise, while in the forests of **Halmahera**
and **Ceram** there are flocks of white cockatoos and
brightly coloured parrots – although the illegal trade
in birds is fast reducing the population.

The two provinces that cover the region have
just 10 per cent of their area as land, so it's unsur-
prising that many of the activities are marine-based.
Improved flight connections and good dive resorts

▼ *Below: Drying nutmeg
and cloves in the sunshine
on Tidore Island.*

facilitate exploration of the underwater, and the annual Ambon Race Week in August culminates in the Darwin to Ambon Yacht race.

AMBON

Arrival at Ambon, the best-known of the Maluku islands, is spectacular. Planes fly in low over ancient volcanoes before a final approach over Ambon harbour. The airport is a 30–40min taxi ride from town, skirting the sea most of the way, or as a pleasant alternative you can cross the bay by ferry.

Ambon Town

Ambon Town is the administrative and business hub of Maluku. If you are spending a day or two here, **Siwalima Museum** offers a good introduction to the history and culture of Maluku. The huge **Pattimura monument** commemorates one of Indonesia's early independence fighters, born in neighbouring Saparua; more impressive and with good views is the **monument to Martha Christina Tiahahu,** also a freedom fighter.

Outside Ambon Town

Just outside town is a beautifully maintained **World War II cemetery** with graves of allied servicemen who died during the fighting. **Waai**, on the northeast coast, has an underground sacred spring, home to huge, semi-tame eels and carp fed by shrine priests. Nearby **Honimua** is a departure point for ferries to **Seram,** where Manusela National Park offers some adventurous trekking. **Soya Atas**, easily reached in the hills above Ambon, is a former capital of the island with interesting megaliths and sacred standing stones, and a stone water container which – according to local legends – never runs dry. Wander through the orchards near the village to see the variety of fruit trees grown here – including the huge jackfruit, sweet-scented cloves, and purple-skinned mangosteen – and the infamous durian from here are said to be exceptionally tasty. Near Namalatu on the south coast is Pintu Kota, a natural arch in the sea cliffs. From the viewpoint on the cliffs are magnificent views along the coast and out to sea.

SPENDING MONEY

The best way to obtain rupiah is to use ATMs, which are widely available even in small towns. Carry plenty of rupiah with you, especially smaller denominations, as these are hard to come by in more remote destinations.

BEACHES

Most beaches on Ternate and Tidore are of black volcanic sand. Beaches in northern Halmahera, around Galela and on the islands in the Bay of Tobelo are pearly white and dreamlike; for sheer beauty the Kai Islands win hands down.

TUAK

The mildly alcoholic fermented sap of various palm trees is sweet and refreshing in the morning but bitter in the afternoon.

MALUKU

Aru Group

Low-lying and swampy, Aru's main claim to fame is as home to several bird-of-paradise species. Their spectacular plumage and courting dances are best seen in the rainy season. Basic hotels are available in the capital, **Dobo**.

Kai Islands

The forests that provided wood for the islands' famous war-canoes (*kora kora*) are gone, but a fascinating culture and beautiful beaches remain. There are mysterious cliff paintings at **Ohoideertawun Beach**, and **Belawang Museum** features trading and war-canoes. Bride prices – still paid – include 14th- and 15th-century cannon and glass beads.

Tanimbars

These islands are famous for *ikat* weaving, carving and golden masks and jewellery (the gold is from the neighbouring island chain, **Wetar**). **Sanglia Dol** village has a stone staircase and a stone 'canoe'.

North Maluku

Halmahera, Ternate and Tidore are fascinating with their dramatic scenery and many different ethnic groups. As with most remote parts of Indonesia, don't expect to dip in and dip out again in a couple of days – these are islands to savour slowly.

At **Hila** (about an hour's drive) is a church dating from 1780 and the 16th-century **Mapauwe Mosque**. Nearby is majestic **Fort Amsterdam**, and along the coast are more, smaller, forts. Further away, the **Hitu Peninsula** is a Muslim stronghold. At **Mamala** village the annual *sapulidi* ritual is held shortly after the end of Ramadan: village youths beat each other bloody, but an hour later no mark remains.

There is good diving at several locations near Ambon, such as at Namalatu on the south coast. The best way to see these sites is to take a dedicated tour on a live-aboard dive boat or base yourself at **Saparua**, an island with some simple accommodation. Sapurua is the main island of the Lease group: come here and forget the rest of the world!

Banda Islands

People visit the Banda islands for a short trip and end up spending days just wandering around, lost in the crumbling echoes of the islands' dramatic past as a centre of world commerce. Visit Fort Belgica on Banda Neira and the old churches with their gravestones of long-dead Europeans, and admire the fine old Dutch mansions, which have lasted longer here than in other parts of Indonesia because no-one has the money to pull them down and start again. The seascapes and sunsets are marvellous, and the snorkelling is magnificent. Climb to the peak of Banda's volcano for the views.

Kai Islands

A few hardy backpackers and birdwatchers visit these islands. Tual (on Dulah/Kai Kecil) is the capital of Southeast Maluku – but don't expect anything sophisticated! There are fabulous beaches such as Pasir Panjang (15 km/9 miles From Tual).

NORTH MALUKU

Like Ambon and Banda to the south, the islands of this chain are littered with ancient forts.

Ternate

The island's capital is **Ternate City**, sprawling along the narrow coastal plain. You can walk from one end of the town to the other in an hour. **Fort Oranje** was built by the Dutch in 1637, and has several old cannon inscribed with the VOC seal. Islam came to Ternate early, and the **Great Mosque** is worth a visit.

The **Kedaton** is still the home of the Sultan of Ternate, and part of it is open to the public; the colours of the palace servants' turbans signify their rank. Offerings are made to the palace spirits three times weekly. The **Crown of Ternate**, credited (like the Sultan) with supernatural powers, is not on public show. The museum has an eclectic collection of exhibits, but opening hours are erratic. Nearby, the huge dark covered market is worth a visit.

The local government has recently woken up to Ternate's important position in the history of science: it was here, in 1858, that the British explorer Alfred Russel Wallace had his revelation that species evolve in response to their environment. The theory was co-published with Charles Darwin later that year. Now, a street has been named after Wallace and a house is being reconstructed on the site where he is thought to have lived.

Around the Island

Ternate is one vast volcano rising to the smoking peak of **Mt Gamalama** (1721m; 5646ft) – a fantastic but tough climb through blasted lava fields. The lower slopes are a green sea of clove trees. Nutmeg is also grown here.

LOCAL DELICACIES

The islanders' diet is mainly fish-based – oddly, local spices are little used. In Ternate eat *kepiting kelapa*, a tree-climbing crab. Try (briefly) *papeda*, made from sago: it has the appearance and consistency of wallpaper paste. In Ambon try *colo colo*, a sweet-and-sour sauce. You may be offered sashimi, slices of raw fish – normally tuna straight from the sea. Delicious!

GRIM SOUVENIRS

You may be offered World War II dog-tags in Ternate, Halmahera and Morotai, grim souvenirs of the war in the Pacific. Some are genuine.

◄ *Left: South of Ternate City, the unfinished Benteng Kayu Merah was built in 1510 by the Portuguese.*

▲ *Above: The view up to Mt Gamalama in the centre of Ternate Island.*

A short walk to the west of town is **Fort Kalamata**, or **Kayuh Merah** ('red wood'); here sunset offers beautiful views towards Tidore and Maiara. The lovely **Danau Laguna**, its surface covered by lotus flowers, is said to be inhabited by a sacred crocodile. The road goes straight through the remains of 16th-century Portuguese **Benteng Kastella**. Beyond, **Sulamadeha** has a black sand beach with safe swimming (crowded at weekends). Take a motorboat to **Hiri Island** (10 minutes), where there is good snorkelling and legends of a visiting mermaid. At **Batu Angus** ('burned rock') are spectacular remains of 18th-century lava flows.

Tidore and Halmahera

A beautiful 45min boat ride from Ternate's Bastiong Harbour, the 'capital' of Tidore – **Soa Siu** – is no more than a village. Fewer relics survive here than on Ternate, although there is an old fort above Soa Siu and another near **Rum**, the arrival point from Ternate. **Halmahera**, the largest island in North Maluku, was once the clove sultanate of Gilolo. Little remains of Halmahera's past; most visitors are ornithologists or anthropologists. Halmahera is currently only accessible by boat. The highest point on the island is Mt Gamkonora (1635m; 5364ft), which had a major eruption in July 2007.

At **Kao Bay** see the wreckage of Japanese vessels bombed during an epic World War II battle. **Tobelo** is a trading port with one of the best traditional markets in Maluku; the town is the largest on Halmahera. Offshore is **Tagalaya Island**, with some good diving. Around **Galela** (in the northeastern part of the island) are pristine white sand beaches, more volcanoes and the beautiful Lake Galela. Nearby is a World War II Japanese airstrip, with the runway made of crushed coral; it's now a banana plantation. The bird life is fantastic, with many hornbills, cockatoos and parrots.

GETTING THERE AND AROUND

By air: **Ambon** is the main gateway to the region: there are daily flights from Jakarta via Makassar in South Sulawesi, and from Manado in North Sulawesi. There are also services from Ambon to Banda and to **Tual** in the Kai Islands and then on to **Tanimbar**. Leave yourself a spare day when returning to Ambon from the smaller islands.

By road: Roads in Ambon, Saparua and Ternate are surprisingly good. Elsewhere be prepared for unsurfaced roads and makeshift bridges. There are virtually no roads (or cars) in the Banda Islands. Much inter-island travel throughout Maluku and coastal areas of Papua is accomplished by motorized canoes called 'johnsons' (after the principal make of outboard motor). They run regular routes between coastal settlements, or they can be hired; private hire is expensive.

Cruising: Several cruise ships and live-aboard boats operate around the Maluku islands, mostly operating out of Bali. Contact www.songlinecruises.com or www.eastindonesiacruises.com for schedules etc.

By sea: Taking a passenger ferry between the islands is a good way to experience Indonesian culture. *See* www.pelni.co.id for schedules.

WHERE TO STAY

There are an increasing number of tourist-class hotels and dive resorts, including on Ambon, Saparua, Halmahera and Ternate. Elsewhere, expect more simple lodgings –

some of them clean and charming. Expect to eat fish, fish and more fish.

Ambon
Swiss Bel-Hotel Ambon, Jl Benteng Kapaha, tel: 0911 322 888.
Grand Hotel Soya, Jl Cendrawasih, tel: 0911 353 463.
Hotel Amans, Jl Pantai Mardika, tel: 0911 353 888.
Hotel Tirta Kencana, Jl Raya Amahusa, tel: 0911 351 867. By the beach, good service.
Maluku Divers Resort, tel: 0911 336 5307, www.divingmaluku.com

Saparua
Cape Paperu Resort has bungalows in dreamy gardens with good diving nearby; www.capepaperu.com
Putih Lessi Indah is simple but perhaps the most peaceful place you'll ever visit; tel: 0812 4748 6647, www.sites.google.com/site/putihlessiindah/

Ternate
The large and well-appointed **Amara Bela Hotel** is a surprise here; tel: 0921 326 500, www.belainternationalhotel.com

Halmahera
Weda Reef & Rainforest Resort, tel: 0812 443 3754, www.wedaresort.com Set up by a British couple to help preserve

nearby rainforest and reefs.

Banda
Hotel Delfika, Jl Ratu Liliselo, tel: 0910 21027, is a delightful place, though simple. There are no restaurants on Banda – the guesthouse will cook freshly caught fish for you.

Kai Islands
There are small guesthouses in Tual, and beach cottages at Pasir Panjang. Coaster Cottages and Savannah recommended.

TOURS

The easiest way to visit Maluku is to join a tour, especially a cruise ship or live-aboard dive boat. Contact Maluku Divers at www.divingmaluku.com for tour details.

DIVING

There is good diving throughout Maluku. The best option remains to follow the programmes of live-aboard dive boats or dive resorts.

SHOPPING

Ambon has the best handicrafts: intricate ships made from cloves, mother-of-pearl collages, weavings and primitive carvings from **Tanimbar** and **Wetar**. Woven baskets can be bought on all the islands, with pottery in **Kai Besar** and the **Lease Islands**.

AMBON	J	F	M	A	M	J	J	A	S	O	N	D
AVERAGE TEMP. °F	82	82	82	80	80	78	78	78	78	80	82	82
AVERAGE TEMP. °C	28	28	28	27	27	26	26	26	26	27	28	28
RAINFALL in	5	5	5	11	20	25	24	16	9	6	4	5
RAINFALL mm	127	119	135	279	516	638	602	401	241	155	114	132
DAYS OF RAINFALL	12	13	13	12	19	21	22	21	16	10	10	13

9
Papua

Indonesia's final frontier and one of the last great wild places in the world, Papua (formerly Irian Jaya) is the western half of New Guinea, a land of snow-topped mountains and huge swamps, of dry savannas and dense jungles where kangaroos clamber through the trees and birds-of-paradise conduct ritual dances. Off the north coast are fine coral reefs and beaches, while inland, in national parks like Lorentz – topped by the massive Puncak Jaya – and Wasur, are birds and other animals found nowhere else in the world. Administratively, the region is divided into Papua, with its capital at Jayapura, and West Papua, whose capital is Manokwari.

Anthropologists estimate there are at least 250 different tribal groups in Papua, each with its own distinct language, including the Dani of the Baliem Highlands and the Asmat, famous for their carvings. Papua's people are Melanesian and, despite the influx of settlers from overcrowded Java and the influence of missionaries and teachers, many tribes hold to their traditional lifestyles. The most serious current threat to both people and wildlife is the virtually uncontrolled plunder of seas, forests and minerals by mulitnational companies.

BIAK AND SURROUNDS

Biak, off the northwest coast, is a good starting point for Papua, with great island-hopping possibilities. The main town – also called Biak – is an Indonesian naval base and a centre for the fish trade, including tuna-processing and oyster-beds. Reefs around Biak Island are as rich as anywhere in the world, with many virtually untouched. Avoid the rainy months of Aug–Oct when surface run-off lowers visibility.

CLIMATE

Plan visits to the **Jayapura area** from Apr–Sep, when it is less likely to be rainy. The **Central Highlands** are cool all year round, with frequent rain. The **south coast** is coolest from Jun–Sep and wettest from Jan–May.

◄ Opposite: A typical Dani compound in the upper Baliem Valley.

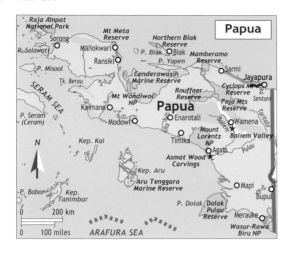

Papua

Bosnik (18km/11 miles east of Biak town) has a white sand beach and views to the Padaido Islands. Charter an outrigger canoe to the islands for wonderful snorkelling. En route to Bosnik, stop off at Telaga Biru, a beautiful blue lagoon in a cave.

Six kilometres (4 miles) east of Biak is the huge **Japanese Cave**, used as a fortress by the Japanese during World War II – until the Americans bombed it, killing the 3000 troops sheltering inside. There is a war memorial nearby. Korem is a bumpy one-hour journey to the island's north coast through jungles and mountains. Pearl-fishers operate in Korem Bay.

The Bird's Head and Raja Ampat

Still teeming with wildlife, amongst the most visible of which are mammoth, colourful butterflies, the Bird's Head peninsula offers adventure – but with some home comforts in the main towns at least. This is part of the province of West Papua, where the main city – Manokwari – lies along Dore Bay, a natural harbour studded with tiny islands. Below the water are the remains of Japanese wartime ships, now offering shelter to a variety of marine life and some interesting wreck-diving. Inland is the Arfak Mountain range, one of the best bird-watching areas in West Papua and also home to magnificent butterflies. Trekking here is still adventurous – be prepared for long hikes in rough terrain with no tourist facilities.

It's an easy journey to the fabulous Raja Ampat islands, where there are several excellent and well-managed dive resorts – or you can visit them from live-aboard dive boats. Alternatively, just lie back in a hammock outside your lodge on the glorious white sand beach, next to the turquoise water, and forget the rest of the world exists.

DON'T MISS

** **Biak**: also called Kota Karang – 'City of Coral' – with unspoilt offshore reefs.
*** **Raja Ampat National Park**: fabulous sandy beaches, good bird life and magnificent reefs.
*** **The Highlands**: home of the fascinating Dani people and dozens of other tribes.

THE NORTH COAST
Jayapura

Jayapura is the gateway to the highlands of Papua. There are flights to all main points from here, and (compulsory) police travel permits (*surat jalan*) can be arranged for trips to the interior.

Museum Negeri (Jl Raya Sentani in Waena suburb) has traditional weapons, shell money, looms and stuffed birds-of-paradise. The museum shop sells a small range of handicrafts.

Around Jayapura

Abepura – home of Cendrawasih University – is 15 minutes from Jayapura. Visit the anthropological museum here, with its wonderful carvings and musical instruments – the most comprehensive collection of Papuan arts in one place.

The village of Hamadi saw the Allied landing in 1944. A couple of rusting tanks still sit on nearby beaches. MacArthur's campaign HQ was at nearby Base G, now the Tanjung Ria Beach Resort, with good water-sports facilities. 'Asmat carvings' on sale here are actually made in nearby Sentani. Above the city is 'Skyline Hill', with beautiful views of the bay; Hindu and Buddhist temples are situated here.

Near the airport, Sentani is very relaxed with a range of small hotels and guesthouses, although the mosquitoes are particularly hungry here. Climb the hill at Doyo Lama (a 10-minute drive southwest of Sentani) to see a group of over 70 standing stones, some engraved with human figures, or Mt Ifar to the northeast to visit the MacArthur Monument. Lake Sentani has fishing and weaving villages on stilts around its shore. Hunt out local carvings and pottery.

THE SOUTH COAST
The Asmat Region

Home of the Asmat tribe, once notorious cannibals. Access is via Agats, a small town connected by wooden boardwalks across the swamps, with a world-class museum of carvings and other local artefacts. Only plan river trips into the interior if you have time, money and patience. This is the place for genuine Asmat art – local Catholic priests

▲ *Above: Lake Sentani, with its scattering of small volcanic islands.*
◀ *Opposite: A spotted cuscus in the Jayapura region.*

THE BIRD'S HEAD

In 2007 the western part of Papua was designated a separate province, with Manokwari as its capital. This is the gateway to more islands and forests, with some excellent bird-watching.

THE INTERIOR

Travel in the interior of Papua has loosened since the Indonesian government allowed provinces more autonomy after 2001. However, expect very basic travel facilities – come armed with mosquito repellent and a strong sense of adventure! A travel permit is essential.

PAPUA

BALIEM CULTURAL POINTERS

- Women with finger-joints missing have not had a horrible accident. This self-mutilation (now declining) marks a death in the family.
- Pigs remain an indicator of wealth in the highlands. Women in remote villages will suckle piglets and cuddle them at night to keep them warm.
- Men sleep in a separate men's house, complete with their enemies' smoked remains and weapons.
- Sweet potatoes, not rice, are the staple in the highlands; the neatly tended fields are everywhere.

have been working with carvers for years. Buy fantastic pieces for a fraction the price you would pay in Bali.

Timika is the other gateway to the south, with good views of the Carstenz mountain range and access – with difficulty – to the Lorentz World Heritage Site. The range includes Puncak Jaya, the highest mountain in Indonesia at 5040m.

Wasur National Park

Kangaroo, deer and wild pigs roam across the swampy savanna, while bird life in the open eucalyptus forests and coastal woodland is excellent. Termite mounds stand up to two metres high. The park is only a 30-minute drive from Merauke; there are small guesthouses in the villages.

The Highlands ★★★

The Dani of the Baliem Valley (known to the outside world only in 1938) are the best-known of dozens of tribes in the high mountains of central Papua. You won't see many people nowadays wearing the traditional penis gourd (*koteka*) or grass skirts, other than for tourist shows. The women still carry goods in orchid-fibre string bags on head-straps and the fields are still worked with stone tools. Tribal warfare continues. If your guide changes your trekking route and won't say why, possibly two tribes are in dispute on the path ahead.

Wamena and the Baliem Valley

A 50-minute flight from Jayapura, Wamena sits over 1600m (5250ft) above sea level in the high, wide Baliem Valley. It consists mostly of government and missionary offices with some small hotels and shops. Although it is the major tourist destination in Papua, even at peak season it is not busy.

The daily market is the focal point, patronized by Dani tribesmen and traders from the coast and beyond. The Dani live in round, thatched houses in fenced compounds. Villages close to Wamena have become commercialized, especially Akima (Momi) with its smoked mummy of a former tribal leader. (Other villages with smoked ancestors are Jiwika, Kimbim Pommo and Wasalma.) There are well-organized treks lasting from a few hours to several days. One of the most popular is the trek to Lake Habbema and Mt Trikora.

▼ *Below: Young Dani men in traditional costume.*

GETTING THERE AND AROUND

By air: Fly to **Biak** or **Jayapura** from Jakarta, Makasar or Bali, or from Papua New Guinea. Jayapura is a full day's journey and two time zones from Jakarta. Centres served from Jayapura and Biak include **Wamena**, **Agats** and **Merauke**. Always reconfirm your departure upon arrival.

WHERE TO STAY

The hotel sector has seen considerable development over the last few years, with most of the larger towns now boasting at least one international standard hotel.

Biak
Intsia Hotel, Jl Wolter Monginsidi 14.
Hotel Arumbai, Jl Selat Makassar 3, tel: 0981 21835, www.arumbaihotel.com

Jayapura
Swiss Belhotel, Jl Pasifik Permai, tel: 0967 551 888, www.swiss-belhotel.com
Aston Jayapura Hotel, Jl Percetakan Negara 50–58, tel: 0967 537 700, www.astonjayapura.com
Hotel Horison, Jl Percetakan Negara 11 no. 2, tel: 0967 522 345, www.horison jayapura.com

Sentani
Hotel Sentani Indah, Jl Raya Hawaii, tel: 0967 591 900, www.sentanihot.com
Reasonable hotel with pool.
Travellers Hotel, Jl Kemiri Raya 282, tel: 0967 582420.

This is a large, international-standard hotel.

Merauke
Swiss-Belhotel Merauke, Jl Raya Mandala, tel: 0971 326 333, www.swiss-belhotel.com
Hotel Nirmala, Jl Raya Mandala 66, tel: 0971 321 849.
Hotel Asmat, Jl Trikora 3, tel: 0971 321 065. Good budget choice.

Wamena
Hotel Baliem Pilamo, Jl Trikora, tel: 0969 31043, www.baliempilamohotel.com
International-standard hotel in the centre of Wamena. Ask about staying in a **Dani village**. The **Lauk Inn** is a guesthouse in **Yiwika** popular with independent travellers.

Fak Fak
Hotel Grand Papua, Jl Panjaitan 1A, tel: 0956 24695, www.hotelgrand papua.blogspot.co.uk

Manokwari
Swiss-Belhotel Manokwari, Jl Yos Sudarso 8, tel. 0986 212 999, www.swiss-belhotel.com
Mansinam Beach Resort, Jl Pasir Putih 7, tel: 0986 213 585, www.hotelmansinam beach.com
Aston Niu Manokwari, Shogun Hill, Jl Esau Sesa Blok B, www.aston-international.com

Raja Ampat Islands
One of Indonesia's best places to go diving, and a real

'get away from it all' destination. Try the award-winning **Misool Eco Resort & Conservation Centre**, located in idyllic islands, info@misoolecoresort.com www.misoolecoresort.com
Raja4Divers is on another island, tel: 0811 485 7111, www.raja4divers.com
Papua Paradise, www.papua paradise.com

SHOPPING

In **Jayapura** the Madinah Art Shop on Jl Perikanan is worth a look. There are several art/souvenir shops in **Hamadi**. In the **Baliem Valley** seek stone axes, cowrie-shell necklaces, string bags, penis gourds and woven baskets. Papua has an illegal bird trade; don't buy any bird-of-paradise skins.

TOURS AND EXCURSIONS

Guided tours with a knowledgeable guide can be arranged through www.papua-adventures.com
The Papua office of **Adventure Indonesia** is at Jl Trikora 2, Wamena, www.adventureindonesia.com
Biak Diving, Jl Imam Bonjol 11a, tel: 0981 26017, runs dive tours around Biak.
The Bali-based firm **SeaTrek** does cruises and live-aboard dive safaris around Papua, tel: 0361 270 604, www.seatrekbali.com
Siam Dive'n'Sail is based in Thailand, but with good Indonesia tours too. See www.siamdivers.com

Travel Tips

Tourist Information

Some useful websites are given below. The official government tourism website – which has good information – is www.indonesia.travel For more helpful tips, visit www.indonesia-tourism.com In addition, www.java. uluwatu.org is good on Java; www.baliexpat.com focuses on Bali; www.east-indonesia.info is good on eastern Indonesia; and www.expat.or.id has helpful tips on Indonesia generally. As with other parts of the world, www. tripadvisor.com and www. virtualtourist.com are useful, though beware false reviews. There has been a dramatic improvement in hotel provision in recent years, with international chains putting good hotels in even remote provincial towns (e.g. Ibis, Novotel, Sahid, Swiss Bel-hotel, Aston International). Some excellent local enterprises are promoting themselves through the web, for example www.gunung-leuser-trek.net has good trekking in northern Sumatra, www.kompakh.org organizes visits to West Kalimantan, and www.adventure indonesia.com is good for off-the-beaten-track tours. Some national parks have good websites, for instance Bunaken (North Sulawesi), Rinjani (Lombok) and Komodo. Most towns now offer Internet cafés (*warnet*), and Wi-Fi is widely available in urban areas, though still restricted outside the towns – don't rely on getting a connection. Mobile phone coverage is ubiquitous and incredibly cheap if you buy a local SIM card – you'll be offered one as you arrive at the airport, or there's always a place to buy one just round the corner from your hotel.

Entry Documents

Visitors from many countries do not require a visa in advance in order to enter Indonesia – you pay for one on arrival. You need to check regulations with the Indonesian Embassy where you live. Even if your country of nationality is on the list for visa-free entry, you must ensure that your passport is valid for at least six months from your date of arrival. Visitors from other nations need to get a visa in advance, available from the nearest Indonesian consulate or embassy.

In 2012 the visa fee for one month was US$35. It is apparently possible to extend this for a further month in-country but it is not straightforward – most people use an agent. If you apply in advance with a sponsor's letter, you can get a socio-cultural visa which allows stays of up to six months via a complicated in-country extension procedure.

If you travel to remote areas (especially in Papua)

you may need to produce a passport photo to accompany some form or another, so take a few with you.

Customs

These are relaxed on the way into Indonesia, although can be stiff when returning to your home country because of fears of the Southeast Asian drugs trade. On the way in there are reasonable allowances for tobacco, drink, perfume, etc. If you need to take medicine with you, make sure that you have also a note from your doctor. Be careful about the souvenirs you buy. Many endangered species are openly traded, albeit illegally, but could land you in trouble if you try to bring them home – for instance turtle shells and bird-of-paradise feathers.

Health Requirements

Health services are improving and even small towns have well-equipped medical clinics which can resolve minor issues. There are excellent hospitals (private) in the cities. You should have good, comprehensive health insurance which includes a medivac option.

Your health documentation will not be checked on entry, but it is advisable to check well in advance with your GP's surgery which vaccinations are currently recommended: particularly hepatitis, paratyphoid, and typhoid. You should be up

to date with your tetanus immunization. Malaria is present in some areas so, if advised, take your anti-malarials before you leave and remember to complete the programme.

Air Travel

There is an excellent network of low-cost air carriers, and air travel around the archipelago is cheap, convenient, efficient and safe. The main international airports are Soekarno-Hatta in Jakarta and Ngurah Rai in Bali. Others are Polonia (Medan), Juanda (Surabaya), and Balikpapan (East Kalimantan).

The state airlines are Garuda Indonesia and Merpati Nusantara. Other airlines are Air Asia, Mandala, Lion Air and Batavia Air, and there are many others serving a small number of destinations. Try to use the more established airlines if you can – they have a better safety record.

Road Travel

Except for buses, metered taxis and some (rare) car hires, you have to bargain beforehand for all road journeys. In Indonesia road traffic drives (officially at least) on the left.

There are various car-hire companies in and around the major population centres, amongst them firms familiar to Western travellers such as Avis. You will need an International Driver's Licence. Except in Bali and

Lombok, it is best to hire a car with a driver. It costs little more, and it is much safer as well as being less hassle.

In some areas you can hire a motorbike for the day or week; again, you will need an International Driver's Licence (with the appropriate motorbike stamp). If you see men on motorbikes loitering about at road junctions and transport terminals, they may well be *ojek* drivers, offering a motorcycle taxi service. They will normally have a spare helmet, and are generally safe drivers. They offer a cheap and efficient way of getting around where there is no public transport. Most drivers of cars and motorbikes in Indonesia do not hold insurance.

Bicycles can be hired in many places.

Taxis: These are available in the larger population centres, but outside major towns they are unmetered: you have to bargain for the price of your journey before you set off. All registered taxis and hire cars have yellow number plates, with black for privately owned and red for state-owned vehicles. If you arrive at any airport other than Soekarno-Hatta (Jakarta) you will need to use a taxi to get into town.

In Jakarta the best taxi company is Blue Bird, which regulates its drivers fairly well. The company also owns the Silver Bird and Golden Bird fleets, which are better still. The Silver and Golden Bird drivers often speak some English. These are not normally available to be flagged down, as they wait at hotels or the airport; however they can be ordered by phone (tel: 021 798 1234). Most other taxi drivers have limited or no English. They are unlikely to know the locations of any but the major thoroughfares, so have a map with you or a good idea of where you want to go.

Buses: Bus services vary from island to island. In Java there are numerous services between the major population centres. The best buses are those for longer journeys which often have air-conditioning, reclining seats and 'in-flight' videos, although the fares are correspondingly more expensive.

Minibuses/*bemos*: These are also called *mikrolet*, *oplet*, *colt*, *angkot* or other acronyms, depending on the location. These vehicles are primarily for journeys between city centres and suburbs or between villages and can seat up to about 10 people, although often they carry more. Their big advantage, apart from cheapness, is that they will let you off anywhere along the route; the disadvantage is that journeys are slow.

Horse-drawn carts, *becaks* and *bajajs*: Horse-drawn carts are available in some cities (even in the Jakarta suburbs), operating rather like taxis; they can carry 2–4 passengers. A *becak* (pronounced 'bechak') is a tricycle whose driver pedals behind you;

they can take two passengers – in Yogyakarta new ones are being introduced with wider seats made for Western bottoms. As with horse-drawn carts, they are becoming rare in larger cities, but you may find one in the suburbs or tourist areas. A *bajaj* (pronounced 'badjai') is like a motorized *becak*, which the driver in front and room for two or three in the back. Noisy and generally belching smoke, these are nonetheless a handy way of getting about for journeys which are too short for a taxi ride.

Trains

Train services run only in Java and parts of Sumatra, and the style of travel varies between luxury and rigour. Night trains run between Jakarta and Surabaya: the Bima, with sleeping compartments, goes via Yogyakarta, Solo and Madiun, while the Turangga does the same route but with reclining seats; the Mutiara goes via Semarang. The Senja Utama is an express running from Jakarta to Yogyakarta and Solo. Longer train rides include a free meal. There are regular trains from Jakarta and Yogyakarta to Bandung; the Parahyangan and Argo Gede run from Jakarta to Bandung (3 hours) and are worth taking for pleasure alone because of the excellent views. Trains often leave on time but are frequently considerably late by the time they arrive. Timetables are available at www.kereta-api.co.id

CONVERSION CHART		
From	**To**	**Multiply By**
Millimetres	Inches	0.0394
Metres	Yards	1.0936
Metres	Feet	3.281
Kilometres	Miles	0.6214
Square kilometres	Square miles	0.386
Hectares	Acres	2.471
Litres	Pints	1.760
Kilograms	Pounds	2.205
Tonnes	Tons	0.984
To convert Celsius to Fahrenheit: x 9 ÷ 5 + 32		

(in Indonesian only but easily understandable), and the site includes online reservation. There's good advice at www.seat61.com/Indonesia

Sea Travel

Pelni is the state-owned ferry line serving all Indonesia's main ports; there are five standards of accommodation, including a luxury standard with en suite bathrooms and in-cabin television. The higher classes of cabin are air conditioned. The ships carry about 1000–1500 people. Look for schedules at www.pelni.co.id (schedules are in English too). There are numerous privately owned ferries – some taking cars, others for passengers only – between the various islands, covering short to long distances; on many comfort is at a premium. There are numerous cruise ships and live-aboard dive vessels operating throughout the archipelago – try www.songlinecruises.com

About 2000 traditional-style Bugis *pinisi* schooners still run between the islands, and for the adventure of a lifetime it is possible to book a trip on one of these. Expect no comfort and do not be punctilious about arrival times – but all that is part of the adventure! These boats are primarily trading vessels, and not very much has changed about them for centuries – except that the sails have been supplemented by an engine.

Clothes: What to Pack

Indonesia's heat and dense humidity make it essential to take a range of lightweight clothing, including a hat for protection against the sun. However, if you are intending to visit areas higher than about 750m above sea level you should also take a light fleece or sweater, while for mountainous areas you should take something even warmer (in the dry season frost occurs in some high villages). A sturdy pair of jeans is also a good idea in case you want to do any jungle trekking or walking – for which you should also bring strong trainers or lightweight boots.

Bear in mind that most Indonesians are Muslim and becoming increasingly conservative, so women in particular should err on the side of modesty when selecting their clothing. Bikinis are permissible on most beaches in tourist areas, but not off them or on beaches mainly frequented by Indonesian tourists; it's a good idea to bring a one-piece costume as well or instead. Shorts, halters and tank-tops should be reserved for the beach or other sports facilities. Men should likewise pay heed to the modesty of their attire, certainly in the evenings; remember that only *becak*-drivers (at the bottom of the social hierarchy) wear shorts and flip-flops, so bring a shirt, long trousers and decent shoes in order to look respectable and for visiting good restaurants. You will not be allowed into nightclubs unless you wear shoes with closed toes (this applies to both men and women).

Money Matters

The Indonesian currency unit is the rupiah (Rp). In 2012 there were Rp. 9610 to the US$, Rp. 15,300 to the £, and Rp. 12,300 to the €. Coins are Rp. 100 and Rp. 500, while notes run Rp. 1000, Rp. 5000, Rp. 10,000, Rp. 20,000, Rp. 50,000 and Rp. 100,000. In remote areas take a supply of smaller denomination notes, since it can sometimes be hard to change Rp. 100,000 ones.

Money is worth a lot more in Indonesia than you're accustomed to: what you might draw from the bank just as pocket-money for the week at home might be enough to support an entire Indonesian family for a month – food, fuel, housing and all. While you may have to grease palms for every extra you require (a better seat, an official form), don't go around flashing your bankroll: you will be regarded as fair game by everyone you meet, and will find yourself paying over the odds for everything.

Tipping: The bigger hotels add a 21% tax and service charge; otherwise (if you're happy with the service) add 5–10% to all of your bills. Taxi drivers need not be tipped, but do round up to the nearest Rp. 10,000. Hire-car drivers expect more. Porters (e.g. at the airport) should be offered at least Rp. 10,000 per bag.

Currency exchange: Normal banking hours are 08:00–14:30 Mon–Fri, 08:00–12:00 on Sat, although branches of banks located in hotels may keep longer hours. There are branches of international banks in Jakarta where you can change your own currency for rupiah; your hotel cashier will be able to do this, as will any of the authorized money changers – of whom there are dozens in Jakarta, fewer elsewhere. A set fee is charged for each transaction, so opt for a large sum each time. Exchange rates vary considerably, and in hotels are much lower than elsewhere. ATMs are widely available, and this method of obtaining money gives the best exchange rate. Before you leave home, inform your bank where you are going in order to try and prevent them from blocking your card (this doesn't always work, however).

Credit cards and travellers' cheques: Credit cards are widely used in Indonesia in towns, although they are still rare outside the major population centres. Because of the potential for fraud, it is best only to use cards only in international class hotels and the better department stores. If you do use one, be wary of the possibilities for

fraud: examine the counter-foil carefully to be sure it shows the right sum, and amend it to obviate any opportunity for later alteration (e.g. the addition of an extra zero). Follow standard anti-fraud procedures in ensuring that people do not disappear behind the scenes with your card, for instance in restaurants, and make sure you keep your PIN secret.

Business Hours

Offices are usually open either 08:00–16:00 or 09:00–17:00, with a lunch break from 12:00–13:00; these hours operate Mon–Fri and, if applicable, Sat. Government offices are open 08:00–16:00 Mon–Fri.

Customary shopping hours are 09:00–21:00 for the supermarkets and department stores in the larger population centres, with truncated opening hours on Sunday. In the smaller cities and towns the shops often close 13:00–17:00.

The opening hours of museums and galleries and starting times of traditional dance performances are displayed in local information centres. This also applies to temple ceremonies in Bali and main tourist centres in Java. Most museums are closed on Monday.

Time

Sumatra, Java, Madura, West Kalimantan and Central Kalimantan are 7 hrs ahead

of GMT; East Kalimantan, South Kalimantan, Sulawesi, Bali and Nusa Tenggara are 8 hrs ahead of GMT; and Maluku and Papua are 9 hrs ahead of GMT.

Postage

Postage overseas is expensive. It's best to carry items home or ship them back. Any valuable item being posted should be registered.

Electricity

Most places use 220–240 volts/50 cycles AC. Plugs are of the two-pronged, European kind. The supply is fairly reliable (although brown-outs are not uncommon) but it is expensive, which partly accounts for the very dim lighting in many places. The wide distribution of low-energy light bulbs has made a big difference.

INDEX

Page numbers in **bold**
indicate illustrations

INDEX